LEGAL ASPECTS OF ANAESTHESIA

DEVELOPMENTS IN CRITICAL CARE MEDICINE AND ANESTHESIOLOGY

Volume 21

For a list of the volumes in this series see final page of the volume.

LEGAL ASPECTS OF ANAESTHESIA

edited by

J. F. CRUL
European Academy of Anaesthesiology

KLUWER ACADEMIC PUBLISHERS
DORDRECHT / BOSTON / LONDON

Library of Congress Cataloging in Publication Data

Legal aspects of anaesthesia / edited by J.F. Crul.
        p.   cm. -- (Developments in critical care medicine and
    anaesthesiology ; 21)
      Includes index.
      ISBN-13:978-94-010-6945-8   e-ISBN-13:978-94-009-1011-9
      DOI: 10.1007/978-94-009-1011-9

      1. Anesthesiology--Law and legislation--Europe.
    2. Anesthesiologists--Malpractice--Europe.   I. Crul, J. F.
    II. Series.
      [DNLM· 1. Anesthesiology--legislation & jurisprudence. 2. Ethics,
    Medical. 3. Malpractice.   WO 233.1 L496]
    KJC6210.A53L44   1989
    344.4'0412--dc20·
    [344.04412]
    DNLM/DLC
    for Library of Congress   89-15578

ISBN-13:978-94-010-6945-5

Published by Kluwer Academic Publishers,
P.O. Box 17, 3300 AA Dordrecht, The Netherlands.

Kluwer Academic Publishers incorporates
the publishing programmes of
D. Reidel, Martinus Nijhoff, Dr W. Junk and MTP Press.

Sold and distributed in the U.S.A. and Canada
by Kluwer Academic Publishers,
101 Philip Drive, Norwell, MA 02061, U.S.A.

In all other countries, sold and distributed
by Kluwer Academic Publishers Group,
P.O. Box 322, 3300 AH Dordrecht, The Netherlands.

PREFACE

J.F. Crul

The topic Legal Aspects of Anaesthesia is still rarely treated in book publications, but deserves increasing attention as more cases of litigation occur each year and anaesthetists also become more aware of the legal structure within which they practice their profession.

I am happy to have been able to obtain the cooperation of experts in this field from various European countries. The contributing authors in this book come from both the anaesthesia and surgery side as well as from the jurisprudential background. As these two fields have their own professional jargon we have been very careful in using definitions, avoiding that a specific term might lead to misunderstanding and confusion. The international authorship did not facilitate this task.

The subject of this book was also the topic of a meeting of the European Academy of Anaesthesiology held at the French Study Center, La Suquette, Saint Vincent le Paluel, held three years before publication of this book. The organizers G. Barrier, J.F. Crul, and J. Lassner felt the need for a book publication presenting the state of the art of anaesthesia and the law in European countries. With the present book this plan has been realized. During the meeting many subjects were thoroughly discussed and the editor considered a number of them as very informative and therefore these were included in this book.

CONTENTS

viii

LIST OF AUTHORS

Prof. G. Barrier
Département d'Anesthésiologie
Group Hospitalier Necker-Enfants Malades-Laennec
149, Rue de Sèvres
75743 PARIS CEDEX 15. FRANCE

Prof. J.F. Crul Ph.D.
Department of Anaesthesiology
University Hospital St. Radboud
Geert Groteplein Zuid 10
6525 GA NIJMEGEN. THE NETHERLANDS

Dr. B. Hallèn
Department of Anaesthesia
Karolinska Sjukhuset
Box 60500
S-10401 STOCKHOLM. SWEDEN

Dr. R.L. Hargrove
Magill Department of Anaesthetics
Westminster Hospital, Medical School
Page Street Wing
LONDON SW1P 2AP. UNITED KINGDOM

Prof. J. Lassner
7, Rue Méchain
75014 PARIS. FRANCE

Prof. C. Manni
Istituto di Anestesiologia e Rianimazione
Università Cattolica del Sacro Cuore
Largo Agostino Gemelli, 8
00168 ROMA. ITALIA

Dr. F. Marchetti
Responsable du Département d'Anesthésie
Laboratoire Janssen S.A.

17, rue Galilée
75116 PARIS. FRANCE
C. Paley-Vincent
Avocat à la Court
40, rue de Monceau
75008 PARIS. FRANCE

Dr. L. René, surgeon
Conseil Départemental de la Ville
Ordre des Médecins
14, rue Euler
75008 PARIS. FRANCE

Dr. C. Roos
Strandvlietlaan 17
1191 CG OUDERKERK A/D AMSTEL. THE NETHERLANDS

Dr. H. Wroblewski
Institut für Anästhesiologie
Klinikum Grosshadern
Marchioni Strasse 15
8000 MüNCHEN. WESTERN GERMANY

PART A. GENERAL LEGAL ASPECTS IN DIFFERENT COUNTRIES

LEGAL ASPECTS OF ANAESTHESIA MISHAPS IN THE NETHERLANDS

J.F. Crul

Every citizen is legally responsible for the actions he/she takes towards other persons. If their actions damage those other persons directly, materially or immaterially, then one is responsible for that damage and should be punished. These principles are laid down in almost all European countries in either civil, penal or disciplinary law codes.

The medical profession is no exception and we find therefore Statutes of Misconduct for the medical profession in every legal system in Europe. Medical specialists have a greater responsibility because of their greater knowledge, skills and experience and usually also take greater risks during treatment of their patients. They are therefore judged more rigidly.

As the profession of anaesthesiologist is a recognized medical specialty in all countries to which the members of the European Academy of Anaesthesiology belong, it is useful to discuss the similarities and differences of the legal aspects of anaesthesia in a representative group of countries in Europe.

The number of malpractice suits in Holland is not as high as on the other side of the Atlantic, but it is on the increase. Those malpractice suits bring out an increasing awareness among the general public about anaesthesia, its risks and rights. This necessitates us to upgrade our knowledge in that field. Nobody is free of exposure to liability, particularly the anaesthesiologists. A legal case may happen only once or twice during our professional lifespan, but if not handled properly, it can ruin the practice and usually also the personal life of the anaesthesiologist involved.

I shall discuss the legal aspects of anaesthesia mishaps in Holland according to the three different systems, namely:

A - civil law codes
B - penal law codes
C - disciplinary law codes

1

A - Civil law codes

According to çivil law in Holland a doctor can be accused of malpractice or of misconduct. In the average case of anaesthesia malpractice is by far more common and only if no contractual relation exists between the anaesthetist and the patient can one be accused of misconduct.

More and more the relation between anaesthetist and patient becomes a contractual one, because both fellow specialists and patients consider the anaesthetist as an independently acting medical specialist. Since 1947 anaesthesia was introduced as an independent specialty in the Dutch Medical Specialists Society and therefore also accepted by the law as a medical specialty.

The main issue in civil law cases is the question whether the nonfulfilment of his duties towards the patient was preventable or not. In other words, could the mishap have been avoided. If it could, liability follows when the following situations exists:
- damage to the patient is proven
- incorrect fulfilment of the treatment is present
- there is a causality link between the two previous ones.

All these three have to be proven before any guilt can be accepted. No punishment without guilt.

Usually the anaesthetist is not bound to guarantee a certain outcome, but on the other hand a minor breach in the correct fulfilment of one's duties to the patient can lead to civil liability. As a yard stick for this correct conduct is accepted the due care, best of knowledge, expertise and skill as is the rule under the majority of his/her colleagues working under similar circumstances.

For both grounds of liability not only damage as a result of an incorrect treatment is liable, but also the lack of an action, which is necessary to avoid damage and also recklessness, which may cause such damage.

Most cases of civil law suits against anaesthetists in Holland are dismissed without trial and the recompensation agreed upon by the insurances companies together with plaintiffs.

Under Dutch law codes the anaesthetist is also responsible for the misconduct of his paramedical personnel working under his supervision. When his personnel is only responsible to the hospital, it is liable for the misconduct or malpractice committed by the anaesthesia personnel. The question of subordination of the personnel is sometimes not clear and brings about a confusion about the subjects of liability.

Some lawsuits have occurred by defective, ineffective or lacking equipment in the practice of anaesthesia. Many more are the result of improper use of well-functioning equipment. Human error is at the base of all these accidents. High quality of inspection and maintenance of equipment is required to avoid litigation.

Since 1980 a minimum package of monitoring equipment is obligatory to be available for each anaesthesia work place. When an accident happens and a legal procedure is started, the anaesthetist has to prove that he used the appropriate monitoring equipment to avoid the mishap.

The availability of the proper equipment is seen as the responsibility of the hospital administration. The anaesthetist, however, needs to have written proof that he explicitly asked for such provisions, but that it was not granted.

Great difficulty has recently been caused by malfunction of complicated electronic monitoring equipment. Liability of this malfunction is difficult to place between producer, hospital technical personnel and anaesthetists. In such cases only proof of due attention to regular servicing is expected from the anaesthetist together with proper checking of the equipment before each operating (anaesthesia) session.

Team responsibility does not exist in Holland. Each partner in the team is fully responsible and separately liable for the damage to the patient caused by the accident. The reason for this attitude is the juridical inacceptability for the damaged party to be caught between the avoidance of responsibility by the individual partners in the teamwork. In the presently increased collectivity of medical teamwork this could happen frequently.

In cases of interdisciplinary responsibility such as positioning of the patient, transfusions and the decisions to continue or break off an operation, the specialist who is most closely related and expert in that particular subject, is taken to be responsible and should make the final decision.

B - Penal law codes
For the anaesthetist the penal law codes number 300-304 and 307-309 can be applicable. They define the liability and punishment for assault and battery and for culpable homicide or corporal damage.

As this is almost inclusively present and proven in every operation or anaesthesia the doctor is only not culpable, if the act was performed for the cure or saving of the life of the patient. When this is performed "lege artis" the law is not applicable.

If, however, the anaesthetist causes severe damage by serious negligence, lack of knowledge or experience he becomes accusable according to the penal codes.

For the proof of guilt it is not only sufficient to indicate that the anaesthetist should have handled the procedure differently according to objective norms, but also that he <u>could</u> have acted differently but nevertheless did not do so, without justification by other exclusion criteria. The high court deemed a severe breach of duty necessary to make an anaesthetist personally reproachable for his actions. In French legal language it sounds "une méconnaissance de ses pouvoirs".

C - Disciplinary law codes

Here the object of liability is not the personal satisfaction or recovery for damage of the patient in the first place, but the breach of the high level of professional quality of care of the anaesthetist. The malpractice must have shaken the faith in the high standard of care of the profession. The disciplinary cases are brought before the disciplinary law court, consisting of both lawyers and medical practitioners.

Application of disciplinary law suits does not exclude the possibilities of civil or penal law suits. On the contrary, they often lead to these further steps.

The measures taken in case the anaesthetist is judged guilty are: admonition, penalty, reprimand, suspension or total exclusion from professional duties. Injury to the patient is not a necessary requirement for guilt.

Sentences by the disciplinary court are felt deeply by the specialist involved and often lead to the termination of actual practice, particularly when the court judges the fact so serious that publication of the case in the professional journals is ordered.

Actual law suits against anaesthesiologists are still very rare in Holland. Most of them deal with penal law cases of death during anaesthesia. Also most disciplinary cases have dealt with accidents leading to death of the patient. Civil law cases are rare and the majority are handled out of court.

The most frequent risk factors involved in medico-legal cases in anaesthesia are:
- Lack of oxygen delivered to the patient for one reason or another. In this respect it should be remembered that all patients receiving inhalational anaesthesia and most receiving intravenous anaesthesia are given an artificial mixture of gases and vapours to which oxygen is added separately. This administration is sometimes endangered by technical mishaps or human error.
- Absence of the anaesthetist from the operating room during the mishaps. Reaction time to reverse the calamity was then unnecessarily prolonged.

- The use of drugs or techniques which are not fully known or understood by the anaesthetist.
- Inefficient resuscitation -when a calamity has occurred- leading to an irreversible one.
- Lack of or insufficient monitoring of the vital organ functions of the patient.
- Poor registration of facts and actions by panicky behaviour of the anaesthetist.

LEGAL BASIS OF MEDICAL LIABILITY AFTER ANAESTHETIC MISHAPS IN FRANCE

G. Barrier

In France, the basis for doctors' liability lies in three legal rules:
A - penal law
B - civil law
C - deontology code
and in regulations coming from the Ministry of Health.

A - PENAL LAW governs criminal procedures. It defines duties for every citizen, and among them, doctors. Five items of it have a special bearing in cases of anaesthesia- and resuscitation practice.

Article 63: imposes upon everybody the duty of assistance to any person in life threatening condition, except in case of personal danger for the witness of this distress (Good Samaritan Law). A prison penalty and a fine are imposed in case of a breach of duty.

Article 318: the person who has voluntary administered dangerous substances to others will be punished by penalties of imprisonment or fines, correlated to the subsequent degree of incapacity of the victim.

Article 319: is very often quoted in medical malpractice suits: "Anyone who, through akwardness, imprudence, inattention, negligence, unobserving of the law, have committed unintentionally a homicide, or have been the unintended cause of it, will be punished by imprisonment for three months to two years, and a fine going from 1,000 to 20,000 FF.".

Article 320: completes the previous one. If assault and battery or sickness are related to a lack of skill or precautions, the guilty person will be punished with imprisonment and a fine.

Article 378: medical doctors, surgeons and servants, as chemists, midwives, and all others who receive confidential informations on account of their profession or by delegation must keep this professional knowledge secret. Those who (except in a few cases, where it is admitted like some infectious diseases, professional diseases, industrial injuries or civil status) commit a breach of confidentiality will be punished by a imprisonment for from 1 month to 6 months and a fine from 500 to 3,000 FF.

B - CIVIL LAW governs the contractual procedures.

<u>Article 1147</u>: builds the civil medical responsibilities on the basis of a contractual obligation. In case of a breach in contract between the patient and the doctor, the victim must be compensated, when this breach is related to the break of a promise, or delay of the execution, not justified by causes which are irrelevant.

<u>Article 1382</u>: Any person who causes damage to another person is obliged to compensate for this damage when he is responsible for it.

<u>Article 1383</u>: Everybody is responsible for the damages not only caused directly by himself, but also by imprudence or negligence.

<u>Article 1384</u>: Everyone is liable not only for the damage caused by himself, but also by matters entrusted to him, or those which he controls.

C - THE DEONTOLOGY CODE is an internal medical regulation for disciplinary issues. It has a force of law, and is published in the "Journal Officiel de la République Francaise". It is released by the "Conseil National de L'Ordre des Médicins". It was modified in June 28, 1979. This change in the code was the first official recognition of independent responsabilities of anaesthetists since the <u>article 59</u> says that "if many doctors collaborate in a patient's treatment, everyone of them assumes his own responsabilities. This is especially the case for the surgeon and other doctors involved in the surgical team. On the other hand, the assistants of the surgeon are under his authority".

All the other articles are devoted to ethics and regulations for all doctors.

All these laws are mandatory. This is not the case for the following regulations.

REGULATIONS ESPECIALLY CONCERNING ANAESTHETISTS

They are issued by the Ministry of Health, and are only strong recommendations.

The oldest one was released on <u>April 30, 1974</u>.

This one describes the safety rules for anesthetising patients, and prescribes: preanaesthetic consultation, anaesthetic records, pre-, per- and post-anaesthetic surveillance, minimal anaesthetic equipment and rules for the recovery room. A regulation released on <u>September 20, 1974</u> describes the "Hospitalised patients charter" and the rights of the patients in the hospitals.

The regulation of <u>March 23, 1982</u> completes the one of 1974. It is specially devoted to the prevention of anaesthesia accidents and to anaesthetic risks. It emphasizes the role of outpatient preanaesthetic consultation, induction rooms, and equipment. It specifies the limits of liability of doctors in the anesthetic field.

The regulation released on June 27, 1985 completes the two previous ones, and regulates the role of the National Committee of Anaesthesiology, which is a specialists council of the Ministry of Health. It emphasizes the description of, and the organisation in recovery rooms in all French territories.

The last regulation was on October 10, 1985 and relates to equipment and security with anaesthetic gases.

DISCUSSION

The penal procedure is in France of great advantage for the plaintive, as it is free of charge for them. The prosecutor can start the investigation, either after a complaint submitted by the patient or by himself. A special committe suggested that doctors should not be considered criminals beforehand, and be sued purely on legal bases. This proposition was rejected however and now this cheap way of legal procedure is already practiced regularly. The penal court is considered competent, whichever law is infringed. The burden of proof still remains with the patient normally, but the judge lays this burden more and more on the defendant: in this case doctors are in deep trouble. As soon as the doctor is sentenced, the compensation by the defandants follows immediately, without coverage by an insurance as it is the case in civil procedures.

The civil procedure. Civil suits are more numerous than penal suits although the number of the latter ones is growing. They should be based on a breach of contract before they can be considered malpractice. The defaults can be accribed to allegations of:
- defective information
- disregards of standards of care
- imprudence
- lack of skill

They are the most frequent grounds, upon which a sue is submitted. In the case of public hospitals, the administrative court is in charge of this affair, on the basis of "Public Service Liability". After the condemnation of a doctor, somebody (the plaintive or the prosecutor) must contact the local disciplinary section of the National Doctors Committee, known as "Conseil de l'Orde des Médecins" if he wants also a professional penalty.

IN CONCLUSION

In France, in case of alleged malpractice, doctors are sued more and more before the criminal courts as murderers. They have to be declared guilty of a fault, and this fault has to be correlated with the damage, suffered by the plaintive. "Damage but no fault" does not exist in our country. Standards of care in anaesthesiology are given by the regulations released from the Ministry of Health. Although not being mandatory like a law, they are accepted by the court and are applied to doctors, who are sued for malpractice.

JURISPRUDENTIAL ASPECTS IN ANAESTHESIA IN FRANCE

C. Paley-Vincent

In France, the courts which have to judge the anaesthetist's liability look primarily for the relation between doctor and patient. They study the role of each of the partners: the operator (surgeon, obstetrician, etc.), the hospital (public or private) and the auxiliaries who take part in, or replace the doctor. In the case of law suits against an anaesthetist this relationship can be analysed as follows.

1. Anaesthetist-patient relationship

That relationship is different according to whether the patient is treated in a public hospital (1.1) or in a private one (1.2), where the doctor is allowed to do his privative practice.

The implication for a hospital doctor or an anaesthetist working in private practice rests on different grounds and will be handled in a completely different way. However, both can lead to legal actions.

1.1 In public hospitals

The relationship of the anaesthetist with the patient is that of a public agent towards a public service user. There is no contract between them, but only the duty of public service.

Administrative laws are applied. These are much milder for the anaesthetist than those in private practice.

Indeed, the administration of the hospital has to compensate the patient if the fault was made during hospital duties, thus confering the anaesthetists an almost personal immunity. Only in case of a "fault outside of service" the administration will sue the anaesthetist in front of the court.

The liability case will be presented in front of the Administrative Courts, which will condemn only in case of serious offense. The medical intervention is considered wrong only in case of a severe breach in patient's care.

However, a recent change of administrative law now gives a more easy compensation for the damages claimed, because of "failure to the public service". The court will not take into account whether that failure is severe or not. It will judge whether the public service has worked well or not. For

11

instance, a bad cooperation between teams, an intern's mistake, the misappreciation of a dramatic evolution will cause the court to order the patient's compensation, because the public service did not work normally.

1.2 In private practice

As a result of a well-known verdict of the Supreme Court (May 20, 1936) the relationship between the doctor and his patient is founded on the basis of a duty of care. Because of a means obligation the doctor must give the patient cares that are conscientious, careful and in accordance to the present status of medical science.
The patient must prove the default in the received care to obtain a compensation for damages from his doctor. Therefore, the patient must demonstrate the causal bond between the care of the doctor with the damages.
In addition to the duty of care the courts request the duty of information, so that the informed consent of the patient can be obtained before the medical intervention.

1.3 The duty of care agreement

In most cases the patient does not select his anaesthetist. The latter works in tandem with the selected surgeon or in the private hospital, where the patient has decided to be operated on. Because of the lack of an elective relationship, the courts for a long time have not recognized the anaesthetist's liability as a contractual one.
On July 18, 1983 the Supreme Court judged that without a personal agreement between anaesthetist and patient, the surgeon is (through his own agreement with the patient) responsible for the faults made by his colleague, who was called upon to work in his team without the patient's choice. However, this verdict will soon be out of date or, at least, quite limited. It will probably be applied only if the anaesthetist has had no contact with the patient before the operation, for example in emergency cases, as so often in obstetrical anaesthesia. Such events are now becoming exceptional.
The ministerial memorandum of April 30, 1974 recalls that every patient, before being anaesthetised, must have a pre-surgical consultation. This consultation allows the anaesthetist to examine the patient, to read his clinical records, to speak personally with him, so that he can ask him about his past health history. After these pre-surgical consultations, some

complementary tests can be required allowing the anaesthesia to be performed in the best possible conditions.

The agreement, creating the direct and personal liability of the anaesthetist, will result from direct contact between him and his patient, highlighting the independence of his speciality.

As a result, the principles of liability for damage (articles 1382 and 1384-5 Civil Code) that apply in the absence of an agreement, will be restricted to the cases when the patient is deceased and his family brings in claims against the doctor, with whom they have no contractual relationship.

1.4 The duty of information

Among the duties toward his patient the doctor must provide him with information that is "simple, general, understandable and fair", in order to obtain his informed consent before the medical intervention.

Recently, the Supreme Court (March 20, 1984) asserted again the duty to inform a patient about the predictible risks of the anaesthesia. In this particular case there was a choice between a general or a local anaesthesia. This is a typical example, which has to be discussed with the patient. However, this information only concerns "the normally predictable risks" (July 12, 1978).

In contrast, for other types of operations: plastic surgery, abortion, neurosurgery, etc., more complete information is required, "even if the possible risks rarely occur" (November 17, 1979).

This duty of information, that was not often mentioned in the past few years, will probably be more often raised by the courts, namely for analgesic procedures such as epidural anagesia and other treatments for intractable pain.

In the case of minors the informed consent will be obtained from the legal representatives, who authorise the operation of the child. When the child's health and body integrity are at risk to be endangered by denial of such an operation, this denial can be overpassed by intervention by the public prosecutor.

1.5 Criminal action

The patient can select his legal action. For instance, he can lodge a complaint with a Criminal Court, which is often for him the easiest and cheapest way. This criminal action can concern public hospitals doctors as well as private practitioners. It is based on proof of the offence and the causality link between the fault and the resulting damages. The criminal judge will be very strict in his appreciation, the criminal law being always restrictive.

Therefore, a default of information cannot be punished by the criminal courts (November 17, 1969), nor a "loss of chance" that is accepted by the civil and administrative courts.

2. Operator-patient relations in

Most of the judiciary decisions related to the liability of the anaesthetist raise also his relationship with the surgeon, in order to define his own liability, or to the contrary, to establish their joint and separate liability.

2.1 Autonomous activity

The independence of the anaesthetist is now often recognized by the courts. A decision of the Court of Appeal of Aix en Provence (November 26, 1969) has defined for the first time the "specific areas" of the anaesthetist: induction of anaesthesia, conditions allowing surgery, monitoring of cardio-vascular and respiratory status during and after the operation until recovery.

Moreover, since then surgeons have been condemned for not having used the assistance of an anaesthestist (November 26, 1969).

Distribution of the tasks and responsibilities even had repercussions on the main medical insurance companies. In 1969, they agreed to distribute the responsibility between surgeon, anaesthetist and private hospital administration according to the competence of each of them. This agreement reflects exactly the solutions usually accepted by the courts in this matter. According to this some court decisions are mentioned below:

a) Pre-surgical tests
"The anaesthetist must, taking into account each particular case, require the tests that will permit the performance of the operation with the highest security" (February 3, 1969).

"The anaesthetist must examine the record of the patient before surgery and make up as much as possible for the possible deficiences; except in cases of absolute emergency he has the duty to refuse to give anaesthesia to a patient without (even minimal) information. He must oppose a non-urgent operation which is not well prepared" (October 23, 1970 and June 26, 1964).

By not doing so he would deprive the patient of the best chance of survival and would possibly endanger his responsibility (January 27, 1970).

b) Setting up of the patient on the operating table
This is generally recognized by the courts as a duty of the anaesthetist and thus is performed under his responsibility, except if the surgeon has particular requirements (July 11, 1978).

c) Conduct of anaesthesia
Before and during the operation the anaesthetist is totally responsible for his intervention. In this regard, it has been judged that by being substituted by someone else during an operation, the anaesthetist has provoked a dangerous break in the conduct of anaesthesia. The desorganisation as result of this break caused a patient's death (December 10, 1970). The anaesthetist must monitor the effects of the medications which he administers, and this is not a duty of the surgeon (November 26, 1969).

d) Recovery
The duty of supervision of the patient by the anaesthetist in the direct post-surgical period and even after awakening has been often reasserted and very strictly evaluated (Aff. FARCAT Versailles, March 4, 1985). A recent decision even overstretches reasonable limites. It says "until recovery of bowel movements".

3. Joint and separate liability of surgeon and anaesthetist

The Albertine Sarrazin's affair illustrated the will of the courts to maintain a joint liability of the two interventions when the patient's interest is at stake. After this famous writer's death, the Supreme Court condemned both doctors (June 22, 1972), insisting particularly on the notion of a surgical team. One of the members of this team cannot assume ignorance of a fault of the other and protect himself behind his own speciality.
The Court of Paris has also maintained the joint liability of the surgeon and the anaesthetist in cases of failures in intensive care. This was the case in an operation of a woman, who died several days after surgery (June 30, 1983).
Several decisions have condemned jointly both surgeon and anaesthetis for a too heavily loaded operating program, established by the surgeon and accepted by the anaesthetist (February 24, 1977).

4. Anaesthetist-hospital relationship

Many decisions reflect how important a role environmental factors can play in accidents of anaesthesia: badly adapted premises, lack of induction or recovery room, insufficiently qualified staff, deficient equipment, too heavily loaded operating programs.
In a public hospital the administration will be condemned because the service was shown insufficient. A deficiency does not even have to be severe.
In private practice the bad quality of care can certainly engage the contractural liability of a private hospital. The liability of the private hospital will be considered exclusive, when the failures are of a nursing nature and not of a medical nature. For instance, the case in which a sleeping patient fell from a carriage (July 2, 1985).
However, there might be circumstances of joint responsibility between the anaesthetist and the private hospital. In this respect, in spite of memoranda of the administration such as those of 1974 and 1982, the work of the anaesthetist remains sometimes "acrobatic", because of insufficient installations and equipment.
Nevertheless, the article nr. 15 of the Deontologia Code (1979) specifies that "the physician must have for his professional practice convenient fittings and sufficient technical means. In no case shall the physician practise in conditions liable to compromising the quality of care". Therefore, the physician accepting to practise under deficient material conditions could be condemned jointly with the private hospital. For instance, an anaesthetist had accepted a too fast operating pace imposed by the private hospital, where he had a contractual exclusivity in his speciality. Both doctor and hospital were jointly condemned (March 11, 1971).

5. Anaesthetist-auxiliaries relationship

Very strict conditions for a delegation of care are required by the courts. The most frequent decisions concern post-surgical periods, when this delegation is often necessary. But also during operations delegation of care is considered extremely risky.
It was often judged that auxiliaries in public hospitals involved in medical acts beyond their competency fall under the liability of the administration (March 15, 1963). In civil and criminal legal cases many examples of post-surgical monitoring left to an auxiliary have led to condemnation, because of absence of precise and strict orders, incompetent staff, delegation too early after

operation. "The anaesthetist can delegate this monitoring only when other operations prevent him from accomplishing this task personally" (December 11, 1970). Thus auxiliaires must always be considered as having a limited competence and must work under the strict supervision of the anaesthetist and not at their own risks.

Another example is that of mid-wives, who cannot prescribe or perform an epidural anaesthesia in the absence of an anaesthetist (The National Consult of Medicine Paris, January 23, 1980 and March 29, 1979).

The courts are very demanding for a difficult speciality like anaesthesia. The judge should always place the anaesthetist's intervention against the facilities, which he has at his disposal, otherwise he risks becoming irrealistic. These facilities are too often still very insufficient.

DISCUSSION

Wroblewski: Dr. Crul, could you please explain how cases are brought under disciplinary law in The Netherlands?

Crul: When a serious accident occurs in a hospital which may point to a malpractice case, the director of the hospital is more or less expected to inform three groups of persons: the public prosecutor and the police department (particularly when it is probably a criminal act), and the regional health inspector. The health inspector investigates the case and in his judgment a case of disciplinary law, he is the one who acts as the prosecutor. He acts for the patient or his relatives if he feels, that the standard of care and therefore the status of the specialty have been breached. Also the patient him/herself or relatives can bring a case before the judiciary law courts. His/her legal rights are however less well protected and/or supported than those of the health inspector. This weakness in the system is going to be changed soon by a new disciplinary law.

Lassner: I will try to summarize for our foreign guests the main legal problems involved in the practice of anesthesia in France.

Mrs. Palay-Vincent has explained to you that there are four possible routes of claims involving doctors. One is for anyone who commits an act contrary to penal law (code penal). If you violate a patient, who is on the operating table, it is no better than if you do so in your car of anywhere else. If you cut a patient's throat while you are meant to anaesthetize him, it is no better than if you cut his throat on the roads.

The second is the civil law (code civil) which makes no difference between selling a car, which does not run properly and giving an anaesthetic which does not go as it should; you have not done what you promised. You were working under a contract. If an anaesthetist is giving a general anaesthetic, he should provide the patient with unconsciousness. If he does not, he is probably not up to par with his contract. This will be discussed tomorrow.

The third type of claim is against the public administration involved in providing care. In France we have administrative courts which take care of only these matters, and if a patient says that, for example, in a certain hospital the oxygen smells of something other than oxygen, or that instead of oxygen he was getting nitrous oxide, then the hospital should check the pipelines, and if they are found to be faulty, the hospital is involved in improper care of patients. If a nurse rather than a doctor does the pre-operative visit, it is improper organization of the service and it is the public hospital administration which is liable for it. Even in a public hospital things can happen which should not be done by anybody anywhere, and then if they are done by doctors, for instance, leaving during an operation, or going on holiday and leaving everybody else without care, then these conducts are not the general fault of the administration, but the fault of the individual. If these things occur the individual can be taken to task for it by the other courts irrespective of the administrative aspect of it.

Finally, in France, like in The Netherlands, we have internal medical regulation with a board set up for disciplinary purposes, but contrary to the situation in The Netherlands, this board nearly never takes its own initiative. Therefore, only if it is requested to do so, will this "Ordre de Médicin" intervene in matters of care. Usually it is concerned only with doctor's conduct as a colleague; for example, if an anaesthetist hangs up a sign saying "My anaesthetics are the best in the world", he would probably be asked to change his sign and possibly even be thrown out of the profession in the end, if he oversteps the boundary too many times.

This seems quite similar to other countries. The penal law court way seems to have advantages over the others and it is the one patients or claimants are prone to take, because it does not cost anything. All it takes is to go to the nearest police station and say, for example: "I believe that my wife has been killed by this doctor in this hospital", and an investigation will start.

If an investigation is started, the doctor is in deep trouble, because if it gets into the newspapers, he may be ruined forever without proof that anything ever happened. The case may be dropped before even starting, and yet the doctor may be terribly damaged by it. We have tried many times to get this situation changed, and a special commission was set up to do so. It suggested that all claims should first be taken up by an independent body to be studied before any action could be taken. This to avoid such a damaging situation. Unfortunately, this was finally refused on legal grounds, because it would put doctors in a position different from all other citizens. "Why should they be protected when anybody else can be accused of having stolen something and be investigated by the police" was the reasoning. Therefore, this inexpensive alternative of either going to the police or writing to the public prosecutor cannot be stopped at present. We are up against this, and the lawyers do their best to protect the doctors afterwards and earn some money with it.

The largest number of cases in France are penal, which implies that something illegal has been done. The difference between the penal court and the civil court is that the penal court is competent, whenever the law is infringed. It must be something which involves a paragraph of the law books, which has been either overstepped or in which there has been misconduct.

Otherwise there is no case for the public prosecutor. It must, again, be a case of penal law.

Some of the legal bases for prosecutions have been quoted by Prof. Barrier, one being that you have not assisted a person in grave danger, which is a general obligation. If ever you go past an accident without stopping, you can be prosecuted for not stopping and helping, similarly for not helping a patient in the operating room. It is the same law. Another one is that you can commit an offence through surgery or anaesthesia if the patient has not consented to it. It then becomes "grave injury" or "bodily harm" instead of "surgical operation". It is considered an assault and battery. If you make somebody unconscious without his consent you are depriving him of consciousness instead of anaesthetizing him. This is another aspect of the same problem; how can a medical act be considered to come under one of the paragraphs of penal law? If this occurs, then the penal procedure will be started. The problem for the medical profession is not so much that people who have committed such acts are prosecuted, but that those who are only taken to task for liability are sitting on the same bench as murderers, and in the public mind they are equal to murderers.

MEDICO-LEGAL PROBLEMS IN THE UNITED KINGDOM

R.L. Hargrove

Summary

Cases of medical negligence occurring in the British Isles and elsewhere are usually notified to one of the Defence Societies e.g. The Medical Defence Union (MDU), The Medical Protection Society (MPS) or The Medical and Dental Defence Union of Scotland (MDDUS). The majority of cases are dealt with by the first two organisations. Twelve thousand new cases from all specialties were notified to the MDU alone in 1985.

Factors involved in 591 deaths will be looked at and also the possible errors resulting in the 159 cases of brain damage for which there are records.
Problems resulting from the failure of adequate pre-operative assessment will be detailed. Factors influencing disasters occurring during operation include failures of technique, use of unnecessary or over-elaborate techniques, the inappropriate use of drugs and abnormal behaviour of the anaesthetist! Several cases of embolism will be reviewed.
Extravasation of drugs is an ever increasing problem and has become a particular hazard since the introduction of the 'Butterfly' needle.
Litigation involving extradural and spinal blocks is increasing and reflects the widening use of these techniques. Unfortunately, it also reflects the lack of expertise or care that exists in some centres. Patches of numbness, nerve trauma, paraplegia and cardiac arrests have all been notified to the MDU.
Damage to teeth and complicated dental bridge work occurs at the rate of two new cases per week. The majority of these could be avoided with proper care and this aspect of anaesthesia is discussed.

Finally, 'awareness' is the most rapid increasing source of litigation. A recent case was settled in favour of the patient and received a great deal of publicity. Since then, a flood of cases have been notified to the MDU and this is causing great concern. Over 70 cases have been notified in the last three years and the numbers are increasing rapidly. Proposals will be outlined which might help to reduce the future incidence of awareness.

FREQUENCY AND CAUSES OF LEGAL SUITS IN RELATION TO THE PRACTICE OF ANAESTHESIA IN SWEDEN

B. Hallén

This paper is intended to give a short outline of the health care system, a survey of the medicolegal formalities and an overview of the officially reported accidents and complaints concerning anaesthesia, intensive care and related activities in Sweden from 1973 and onwards.

Background

The area of Sweden is about the same as that of France. If you go by jet it will take about two and a half hour from the south to the north and less than one hour to go from east to west.The population is about 8.5 million people out of which 8% is 75 years of age or older. For the moment being the number of aliens is about half a million.

Most people live in the southernmost part and in the regions around Stockholm and Gothenburg leaving the rest of the country sparsely populated. The number of employees is about 4.3 millions out of which 1.6 are to be found under Services, 1.0 under Mining,Manufacturing,Electricity and Water Services and 0.6 in Wholesale and Retail trade, Restaurants and Hotels.The total national disposable income is about 650 000 million Swedish Crowns which is about the same sum in French franc.

THE SWEDISH HEALTH CARE SYSTEM

Sweden spend around 9.4% of its GNP on health and medical Care. In 1985 about 450.000 persons were employed in health services equivalent to about 10% of all employees. In 1987 this figure corresponds to about 315.000 full-time jobs The public medical and dental care is planned and run by the 23 county councils and 3 of the municipalities. Costs are defrayed by taxes to a large extent. The state transfers funds to the councils and the municipalities and the patients contribute directly by modest fees.

There are approximately 25.000 active physicians below the age of 70 in Sweden most of them employed by the County councils. The total number of private physicians who work on a full time basis is very small, only about 5%.

23

The National Board of Health and Welfare

Under the parliament and the Ministry of Health and Social Affairs, the National Board of Health and Welfare (NBHW) acts as supervising agent. There is a special board of scientific advisors connected to NBHW, the anaesthesiological members of which are professors Dag Lundberg in Lund and Erik Vinnars in Stockholm. These scientific advisors may be, but do not necessarily have to be, consulted in anaesthetic matters. Usually medical cases are prepared and decided upon by specialist referees, at least one in most medical specialties.

Anaesthetic practice

The Swedish Society of Anaesthesia and Intensive Care (formerly Swedish Society of Anaesthesiologists) has about 1020 members and the National Board of Health and Welfare in 1988 registers 973 specialists in anaesthesiology.

There are 95 departments of anaesthetics where something between 650.000 and 600.000 anaesthetics are given each year. These are distributed so that there are some 30-40.000 spinals and about 60.000 epidurals and the remainder is made up of various types of general anaesthetics. No official figures exist as there is no compulsory registration requiring anaesthetic statistics to be prepared and centrally filed. The figures given above are based on the knowledge of the number of beds in hospitals and on repeated questionnaires sent to the anaesthetic departments.

The number of laws and regulations set up by the state concerning anaesthesia and intensive care are very few and the practice left at the discretion of the licensed physicians.

THE SWEDISH MEDICO-LEGAL SYSTEM

National Board of Health and Welfare

Since very long all medical accidents have to be reported to the NBHW. A special law requires e.g. hospital management to notify NBHW immediately in the event of any person suffering serious injury or contracting a serious disease in connection with health care. Notification of this kind, which is mandatory irrespective of suspicion of malpractice or negligence is followed by an official investigation. The prime objective is to try to create knowledge, hopefully in order to be able to take preventive measures, but criticism may of course also follow as a result of the reports and investigations. In such a case NBHW acts as prosecutor at the Medical Responsibility Board who then may decide upon disciplinary measures against the person involved.

During recent years there are approximately 350 reports annually relating to the somatic specialties, filed with the NBHW. Some 70-75 of them come from anaesthesia, intensive care and related activities. In the following these cases will be called "Reports".

Medical Responsibility Board

All people working in health and medical care are controlled in their capacity as professionals by the NBHW. If they are critizised as such they may have their case tried by a special Medical Responsibility Board (MRB). If convicted disciplinary measures can be undertaken against them. Registered nurses, physicians etc. may lose their licenses and get formal warnings pronounced.

The MRB is composed of nine members and three personal deputies, for each of them, appointed by the Government. The chairman has to be a qualified lawyer with judicial experience, usually from the court of appeal. Of the other members, one is appointed after nomination by the Federation of the Swedish County Councils, one after nomination by the Swedish Trade Union Confederation, one after nomination by the Central Organization of Salaried Employees and one after nomination by the Swedish Confederation of Professional Associations. The remaining four members are appointed directly by the Government to represent the general public in relation to the health care sector and usually are MPs. As referees or rapporteurs to the board specialists in the various fields of medicine are used.

The basic rule of disciplinary liability is stated in the so called Supervision Act as follows:

"If a person belonging to health and medical personnel intentionally or negligently fails in the discharge of his professional duty and the fault is of more than a minor nature, disciplinary sanctions may be imposed on him. Disciplinary sanctions comprise admonitions and warnings."

The prime concern when implementing this provision is to define "professional duties" of medical personnel, which obviously is a very delicate matter. The more so as the basic rule as phrased in the General Instructions for Physicians Act require every physician to act:

> "... in compliance with science and proven experience, to give the patient advice and, as far as possible, the treatment which their condition requires..."

Obviously such a rule leaves much to be discussed in almost every case.

Entitled to raise questions of disciplinary liability at the MRB is, as already mentioned the NBHW and the patient concerned, or if he cannot personally do it, a close relative. These questions, that have to be raised not later than two years after the event, almost always take the form of complaints and in the following I refer to these cases as "Complaints".

Appeals against decisions by the MRB or NBHW are lodged with the Administrative Court of Appeal in Stockholm, whose decisions can be contested before the Supreme Administrative Court. The decisions of the MRB may be contested by NBHW and the individual complainant and any other person to whom the decision refers, though the last two mentioned may only appeal if the decision was against them.

The largest number of cases comes from orthopedics and general surgery (20%) followed by psychiatry and general practice (15%). About 10% come from each of internal medicine, pediatrics, obstetrics and gynecology, and long-time (geriatric) care. Only relatively few cases are due to anaesthesia and ophthalmology. The total number of cases from the entire medical field filed with the Medical Responsibility Board has risen from about 700 in 1980 to more than 1200 last year. About 60% of the cases concern doctors.

Civil Courts

Of course cases may also be tried at ordinary civil courts where also claims of economical compensation are to be tried. Very few cases actually occur and the amounts accorded for i.e. aches and pains have hitherto been fairly modest. However, there seems to be a tendency by lawyers to encourage patients to take allegations of malpractice to civil courts.

Appeals against decisions of civil courts follow normal judicial rules.

Patients Insurance Scheme

To improve the economical situation for patients who have suffered damage during medical care there is a Patients Insurance Scheme (PIS) financed by tax money and encompassing all citizens. In order to be eligible for compensation the patient's injury or damage should have resulted in at least 14 day's prolonged care and is to be of such a nature that it does not lie in the direction of danger, i.e. it should not be the result of a well known and calculated risk of the procedure. On the other hand there is no need to prove malpractice or negligence of the part of the health personnel nor is there any connections between this insurance scheme and the Medical Responsibility Board. On the contrary the locks between MRB and PIS are almost watertight.

This fact has some consequences: there are probably a great number of cases, i.e. anaesthetic accidents that according to the previously mentioned mandatory laws, should have been reported by the responsible hospital management of doctors, but which are now settled exclusively in the PIS thus leaving the patients satisfied but society oblivious of the actual magnitude of the risk factors inherent in health care.

One example of this is the problem of injuries to the teeth in connection with tracheal intubation. The PIS has knowledge of several hundred cases that have been economically compensated but there is only one or two cases in my entire material from NBHW and MRB between 1973 and 1988. Another example concerns neurological sequelae of various spinal and epidural techniques. There are at least three times as many cases in PIS as in this material reported on medicolegal reasons.

OFFICIALLY REPORTED ACCIDENTS AND COMPLAINTS 1973-1988

Making statistics out of legal suites following anaesthetic mishaps or complaints from patients is liable to a number of possible scientific errors. The material is partly retrospective, it is heterogenous and its completeness can not be guaranteed. In addition it cannot be ruled out that misleading facts are intentionally included in the individual reports. The purpose of presenting these figures is thus primarily to illustrate the medicolegal reality in Sweden of today and not to try to establish any general truth about anaesthetic complications. On the other hand even disparate information may be valuable and add to the safety of our future patients and protect ourselves from unnecessary medicolegal troubles.

During the years since 1975 when I started my work as a referee in the NBHW I have taken part in the inquiries of more than 600 medicolegal cases officially reported and dealing with anaesthesiology and related activities. The cases are derived from operating theatres in 49%, intensive care 20%, general wards 9%, ambulance service 5% and obstetric and emergency each in about 2% each. Such a classification is however by no means clear and absolute as in many of the cases there are multiple complaints or reasons to an anaesthetic complication. 37% of the cases involve the death of a patient, not necessarily caused by any mishap, and a subjective classification yields a further 49% of "major" and 13% of "minor" complications.

There has been a considerable increase in the annual number of cases during the last decade, as is shown by Fig.1 where the year of the event causing the report or complaint is shown. Totally the material consists of 627 cases. It has to be observed that there may be a considerable lag between an event and the filing of a complaint, as a mean this lag is half a year.

The average age of patients is 47 years and the distribution roughly corresponds to that which we are used to se in big anaesthetic departments handling all kinds of surgical specialties. There are slightly more females in the age groups 30 to 50 and more males up to 10 year and between 60 and 80 (Fig.2).

The difference between the number of males and females varies considerably between individual years but there is no trend to be seen. Totally there is a small preponderance of men.

As previously mentioned the material basically consists of two types of cases; complaints filed with the MRB and mandatory reports filed with the NBHW (Fig.3). However, the border between the two types of cases is not absolute: sometimes the responsible physician files his mandatory report in the same time as the patient or his relative files a complaint. In addition, the investigation of NBHW may result in NBHW requiring disciplinary action against a person involved in a case. As a result there is an overlap: 74% being "reports" and 40% being complaints.

Figure 3 also shows that there is an increasing proportion of reports. Although the distinction between the two types of cases is not clear-cut, it is probable that the observation is correct: there has been a new law from 1980 and efforts to get more reports have been made. The new law stresses the preventive purpose of the law in contrast to the earlier more medicolegal aspects and the former obligation to inform police authorities of all reports to NBHW has been abolished.

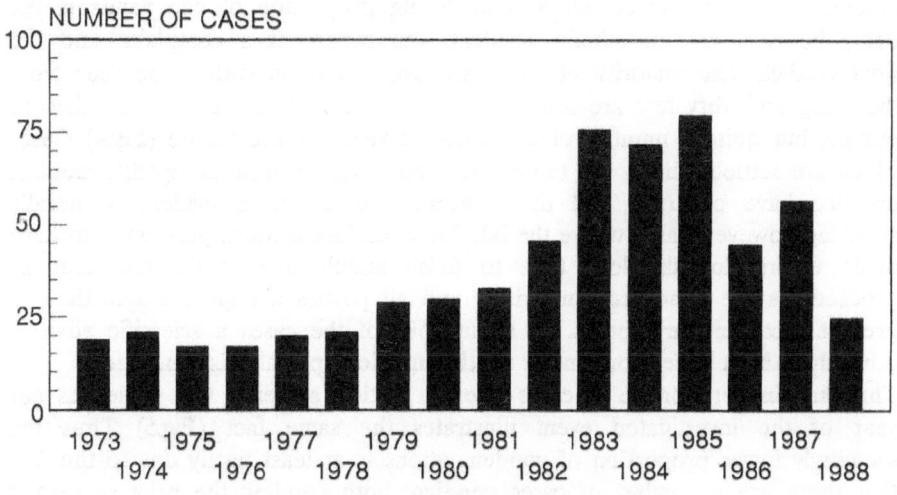

FIGURE 1:   Anaesthetic accidents and complaints officially
reported in Sweden 1973 - 1988

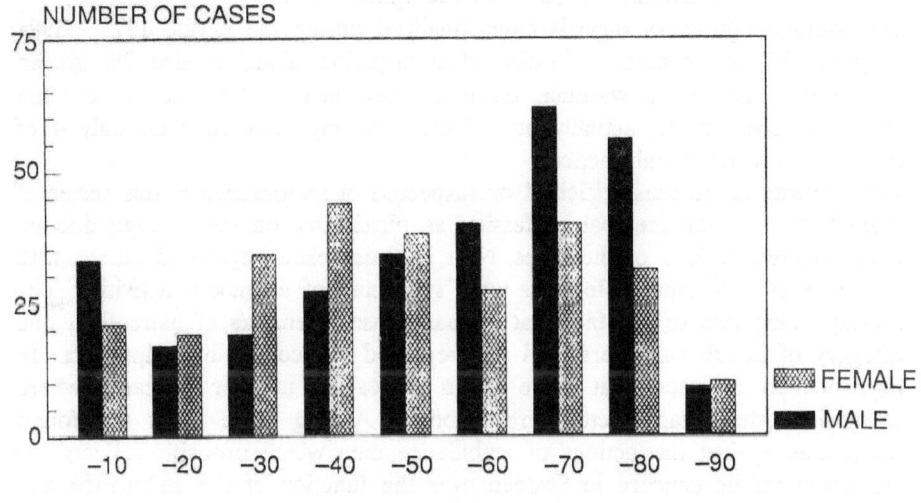

FIGURE 2:   Anaesthetic accidents and complaints officially
reported in Sweden 1973 - 1988

Another cause of the seemingly diminishing proportion of complaints is the delay between an anaesthetic accident, the report of a complaint and the final verdict. The majority of cases are decided upon within one year from the filing and very few are settled in shorter time. As an average it takes 15 months but quite a number of cases take 2 years or even more (Fig.4) Cases which are settled quickly are those where no deviation from acceptable medical practice have occurred and those where malpractice is evident. Generally speaking however, cases where the NBHW considers medical personnel to have made errors do take long time to finish mainly due to the fact that all proceedings are conducted in writing and all parties are given ample time to present facts and arguments. In about 25% of the cases a scientific advisor, other than the referee, from one or another medical speciality is consulted.

The changing proportion of cases where a critical sentence was passed as per year of the investigated event illustrates the same fact (Fig.5) Thus the seemingly lower proportion of condemnations is at least partly due to the fact that there are a number of cases pending, both pending the primary verdict and cases where appeal to higher courts have been made. It may however also reflect an increasing proportion of reports or complaints where no fault of personnel was included.

Cases filed only as reports are criticized in about 6%; those filed only as complaints in 17% and those filed both as complaints and reports in about 48%

The average figures as regards cases finalized during the period 1973 - 1988 are that 88% of the cases were cleared of suspicion of malpractice, 7% got an admonition and 4% a warning. Extremely few anaesthetic cases have been settled in civil courts, actually only 9 cases to my knowledge an only 4 of them got a verdict of malpractice.

The majority of persons criticized or suspected of malpractice in this series of cases belong to the medical profession as physicians, on the average doctors were involved in 77% of the cases. Next in order came registered nurses with 23% and in 17% other categories were suspected of erroneous activities. The overlap being due to the fact that in many cases members of more than one category of health care personnel was reported or accused of malpractice. In Fig.6 it can be seen that there is an increasing number of cases where categories other than doctors are involved. Among these cases are found complaints against the actions of ambulance men which probably reflects the increasing public concern in Sweden over the function of the ambulance and rescue system and it is evident that Sweden has much to learn from e.g. "le SAMU" of France.

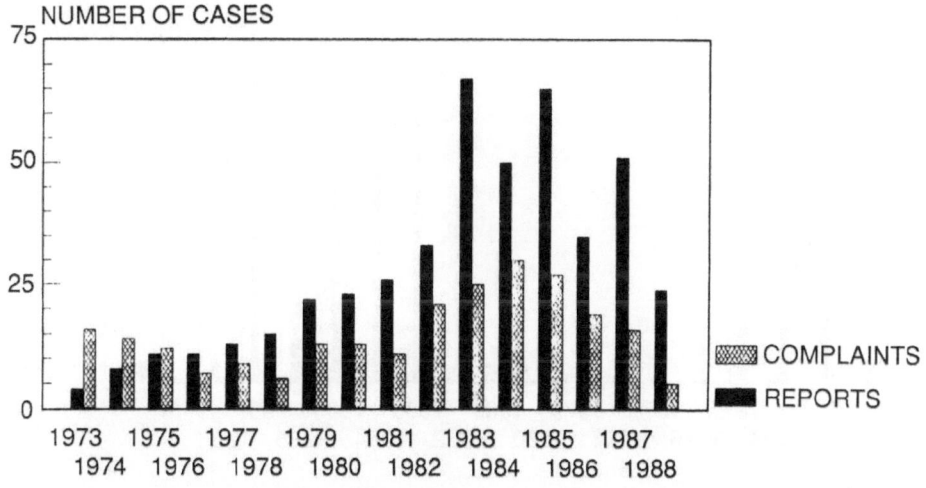

FIGURE 3: Anaesthetic accidents and complaints officially
reported in Sweden 1973 - 1988

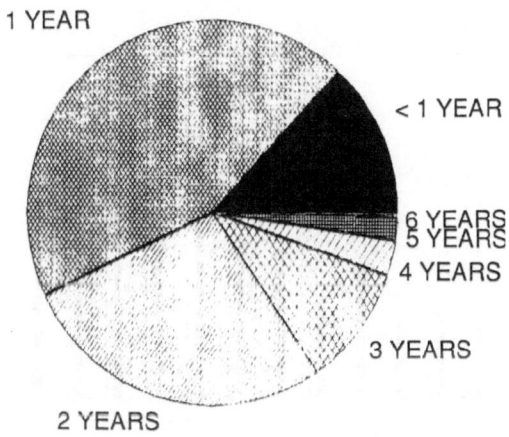

NUMBER OF YEARS BETWEEN EVENT AND
DECISION, PER CENT OF CASES

FIGURE 4: Anaesthetic accidents and complaints officially
reported in Sweden 1973 - 1988

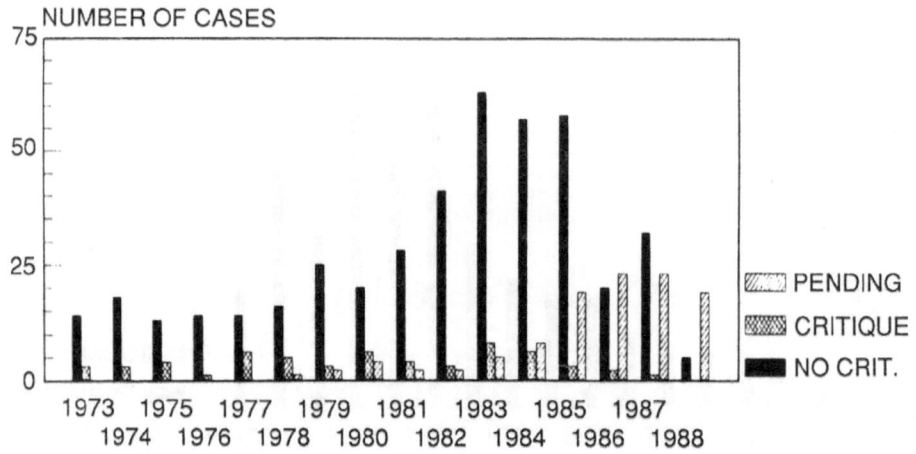

CONSEQUENCES OF REPORTS AND COMPLAINTS
DISTRIBUTION BY YEAR OF EVENT

FIGURE 5:   Anaesthetic accidents and complaints officially
reported in Sweden 1973 - 1988

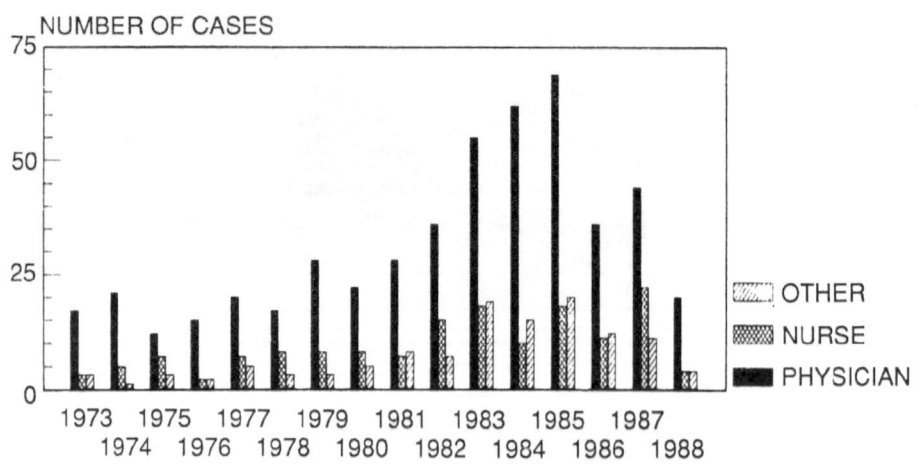

CATEGORIES OF HEALTH CARE PERSONNEL IN-
VOLVED, DISTRIBUTION BY YEAR OF EVENT

FIGURE 6:   Anaesthetic accidents and complaints officially
reported in Sweden 1973 - 1988

EXAMPLES OF CASES AND THEIR LEGAL CONSEQUENCES

Most of the 627 cases collected up to December 1988 are quite individual and trying to put them together into groups results in either very heterogenous or very small groups. Some groups however are easily distinguishable: complications due to central venous catheters, epidural anaesthesia and cases involving pain and insufficient anaesthesia.

Cases concerning epidural anaesthesia or analgesia constitutes one of the major groups, totally 56 cases, 25 males and 31 females. This type of cases tend to increase. Most of the errors are severed catheters. When the doctor in question makes it probable that he has not intentionally tried to pull the catheter backwards through the Tuhoy needle the case is closed without any further action but if it is probable that he has been careless in manipulating, an admonition is given.

There are also a number of neurological sequelae to epidural anaesthesia or analgesia e.g. the so called cauda equina syndrome. In most of these cases no explanation is found but the mere fact that there are unwanted sequelae does not constitute basis for criticism.

Cases involving central venous catheters form another large group, 19 males and 31 females and the frequency of this type of cases also seems to increase. There are all types of complications to these catheters including 17 deaths. Regrettably it seems as if some of our younger colleagues consider introducing central venous catheters to be without great risk and use this technique quite liberally. There is, however, very seldom criticism spoken by any of the two boards.

In contrast to the two aforementioned groups the frequency of cases involving pain and insufficient anaesthesia seems to be more constant during the years studied. Totally 34 cases, most of them being in the form of complaints, have been filed. They constitute major investigatory problems as these complaints often are purely subjective, by definition. The decision whether the doctor has been negligent as regards the pain of the patient thus often depends upon the existence of witnesses and any signs of e.g. stress reactions in the anaesthetic record such as unexplained tachycardia or hypertension. In most cases however no proofs can be presented from either side and most decisions consequently states that words stand against words and thus no disciplinary action is taken.

There are three almost identical cases of neuroleptanaesthesia where the patient woke up after anaesthesia in the operating theatre but relapsed into sleep and recurarization shortly after the arrival in the postoperative ward. In all three cases the consequences were disastrous: two deaths and one serious cerebral damage. The risks of neuroleptanaesthesia, recurarization and the deleterious effect of hypoxia upon the sensibility to carbon dioxide of the respiratory centers is shown. From a medicolegal point of view much discussion has been going on. The first case which occurred more than 10 years ago did not result in anything but modest critique against the county council and its lack of allocation of resources to the recovery ward, but the last case, which is still under investigation, may well end up at a criminal court.

The material contains 42 cases where mixing of syringes etc have occurred. In 12 of these cases syringes with suxamethonium have been erroneously taken to contain physiological saline. The erring person usually have been a nurse or a young doctor who have forgotten to read the labels carefully or properly to sign the syringes. The verdict in these cases almost always is a warning. Similar sentences usually are passed when errors of blood transfusion have occurred.

In general, the severity of the sentence is not dependent upon the severity of the reaction of the patient or the damage inflicted, but only to the fact that malpractice has been proven.

LESSONS LEARNT

Taking part in investigations of anaesthetic accidents is most profitable from a teaching and scientific point of view. Much is learnt about the dangers and pitfalls of anaesthesia that can be used in teaching and clinical work.

The main evidence when investigation a case is the anaesthetic record. A well written record shows the concern and professional skill of the anaesthetist and is a most valuable tool to contradict an allegation of malpractice. However there are cases where the temptation afterwards to improve a poor record have not been resisted, but such forgeries, although not always easy to detect even for a professional referee, seriously damages the position of the doctor.

Anaesthetic accidents, however serious they may be, are in most cases accepted as such by the National Board of Health and Welfare as well as by the Medical Responsibility Board. Insufficient and careless preanaesthetic investigation and preparation however, as well as lack of attention during anaesthesia and recovery, usually constitute reason for verdicts of malpractice.

SUMMARY

The number of officially reported accidents and complaints in relation to anaesthesia, intensive care and related activities in Sweden at present amounts to about 75 per year.

The official medicolegal investigations do not result in formal critique in about 88% of the cases. In about 7% admonitions and in about 4% warnings are pronounced by the Medical Responsibility Board and only in exceptional cases verdicts are passed at civil or criminal courts.

The frequency of official complaints regarding anaesthesia and intensive care in Sweden is at present small, i.e. between 1 and 2 per 10.000 anaesthetics given ! This situation is now changing with the numbers of both complaints and reports increasing. Due to the system with a compulsory patient insurance scheme and mandatory reports from hospital management, a development similar to that seen in the USA is however, not expected.

LEGAL LIABILITY SUITS AFTER ANAESTHETIC ACCIDENTS IN GERMANY

H. Wroblewski

In this paper the question is raised how legal procedures against physicians take place in the Federal Republic of Germany today. We discuss the development at this stage and finally we shall look at the conclusions to be drawn.

In the press we all read the American newsreports, which tell us of a constant growth of actions for damage against physicians, barely affordable insurance premiums as well as spectacular settlement payments to patients. Is this trend towards rising legal suites against the medical profession also manifest in Germany?
Unfortunately I must disappoint you because of the lack of hard figures, which might directly prove this development, figures comparable for instance to the large scale American insurance study of NAIC in 1978. Such numbers and investigations do not exist in the Federal Republic. However, there are in my opinion sufficient indirect hints, which at least indicate a tendency. Forensic physicians (Pribilla) estimate the number of complaints filed at about 1000 to 1200 per year. Ulsenheimer mentions some 100 preliminary investigations by public prosecutors per year during the period of 1977 to 1980 in Munich alone. Weyrs indicates roughly 6000 liability claims based upon medical malpractice for the time from 1970 till 1978, 10% of which are still pending in court. A large insurance company estimates that around 3% of all claims lead to a preliminary investigation by public prosecutors. The Forensic Medical Institute of Munich's Ludwig-Maximilians-University received five orders per year for expert opinions regarding malpractice allegations between 1950 and 1970, 20 from 1971 to 1975 and afterwards 70 orders per year, which constitutes a 14-fold increase. Particularly revealing is Ulsenheimer's statement, observing a 3-fold increase between 1980 and 1985 in attorney retainers for criminal cases involving anaesthetists. Moreover, these retainers equal about 25% of all retainers involving surgical fields, thus indicating anaesthesiology to be a speciality of particular forensic risk-affinity. So far for some hard facts.

Before we return to the reasons for this development and the question of judicial interaction with the medical profession, let us briefly pause for a

38

statement: Even if the American situation is not equaled in the Federal Republic of Germany, neither in terms of number nor amount of financial compensations, a growing tendency towards forensic medical involvement in the wake of accidents can nevertheless be observed. And the end is not yet in sight.

Let me discuss now the different kinds of forensic medical involvement possible after anaesthetic accidents in the Federal Republic. By doing so, it is particularly necessary to explain the relationship between civil litigation and criminal procedures, a relationship basically unknown to the Anglo-American legal system.

Generally an accident can cause a physician's criminal and civil liability, whereby both possibilities exist independently of one another. Civil law is concerned with a patient's damages as personal injury, pain and other suffering. Criminal procedures, on the other hand, involve the right of the citizen of punishment in order to compel socially adequate behaviour.

It may fairly be assumed that the injured patient is more concerned with satisfaction of his financial claims than with penalty of the medical profession. Yet he will frequently file a criminal complaint against the physician, almost as an opening move in his struggle for compensation. Let me try to make this plausible. Such strategy, and so much can be revealed here, primarily exists due to the different burdens of proof in both procedures.

A civil procedure concerns only claims for damages including those for pain and suffering, which the injured patients assert. Both patient and doctor are the only parties in the litigation and insofar masters of the procedure. The maxim of party disposition is applicable: The patient determines the scope of the action, he can extend, reduce and withdraw it. The physician is equally free to make the action obsolete by admitting the claim or settling it.

In essence the patient has two grounds on which to base his claim:
- Either he alleges that the physician did not treat him lege artis, that is his injury was caused by malpractice, or
- he asserts that he was not sufficiently informed about the treatment, the so-called allegation of inadequate information.

Concerning the so-called malpractice allegation the burden of proof rests upon the patient. If he fails to show that the doctor's treatment deviated from medical standards, the action will be in vain and the claim dismissed. In practice producing such an evidence may turn out to be rather costly and time consuming for the patient. Therefore, the uneven distribution of the burden of proof has been loosened somewhat by court rulings. The patient's burden of proof for instance may be facilitated in case of prima facie evidence. Vis-a-vis a physician's gross violation of his documentation duties or an equally gross mistake in treatment the burden of proof may shift altogether, now forcing the doctor to show that he conformed with professional standards. These are, however, only exceptions to the general rule, according to which the burden of proof lies with the patient.

In order to escape those burdens the patient will frequently resort to an allegation of inadequate information. This simply implies that the patient must allege not more than a medical treatment without sufficient prior explanations. The allegation itself suffices to shift the burden of proof of effective information onto the physician. If he fails, he will be adjudicated to pay the damages. Behind this principle stands the German legal concept that every medical treatment is looked upon as on offence of personal integrity. Its wrongfulness is precluded - and the offence remains without sanction - only if it was justified. But this can only be the case when a valid prior consent to the treatment existed. To accept such a valid consent the patient must have been sufficiently informed, that is: he must have been able to make a decision, free of errors. Only under these preconditions will his consent qualify as an effective justification. The necessary information for it must be provided for and - if litigation follows - be proven by the physician.

This has produced extensive jurisprudence since it can only be determined for each case individually, with due regard to the "expectations" of a "average" patient.

Of importance for the scope of the required informations is, for example, the urgency of the operation, or the fact that is was a diagnostic or therapeutic procedure. This legal option to assert civil claims via an allegation of inadequate information now fills whole court libraries. It is interesting to notice that the relevant Higher Court opinions have shown repercussions for the daily life of the anaesthetist. In connection with these problems of information the Bund Deutscher Anästhesisten (Professional body of German anaesthetists) has developed a questionnaire containing 26 questions concerning anaesthesia. The questionnaire is designed to help the physician towards better documentation and information in accordance with judicial standards. Sofar one can clearly speak of a legal interference in medical affairs in the sense that medical decisions are being influenced by judicial parameters. It should be mentioned at this point that the allegation of defective information carries with it some disadvantages. First of all only a limited percentage of cases can be persued in this way. Excluded are emergency operations and those in which the documentation duty was fully complied with. Secondly, the amount of damages to be recovered is somewhat diminished. It is limited to those immaterial damages attributable solely to the omitted information. In short it is more uncertain - but in the end more profitable - to go the malpractice route.

These statements were meant to explain how the assertion of civil claims can entail tremendous evidentiary problems and great financial risks for the patient. This is the key to understand why often <u>criminal</u> procedures against physicians are instituted in the Federal Republic. In order to minimize the risks involved in civil litigation the patient may file a criminal complaint against the doctor. Thus he sets in motion an inquisitorial procedure under the auspices of first the public prosecutor and later the court. Both are the sole masters of the procedure and act according to the rule that only the public prosecutor can bring a criminal case to court. All procedures of admissable forms of evidence must be exhausted to prove the physician's guilt. These may include, among others, the compulsory testimony of witnesses, who are under a legal obligation to testify and may be punished for refusing to do so. It may also include hearing necessary expert opinions. Contrary to a civil action the criminal proceeding is beyond the patient's or doctor's influence from the very moment the complaint is filed. Whenever a reasonable suspicion of an offence as well as a public interest exists, an indictment must follow. Once in court the principle of "in dubio pro reo" is applicable, meaning that doubts concerning causality or guilt will preclude the physician's conviction. If, however, a conviction is reached the doctor faces a fine or detention and/or a prohibition to practise his profession.

At the beginning we have stated that civil and criminal liability does not exclude or prejudge each other but exists independently. In practice, however, the beginning of a criminal investigation will benefit the civil action, since civil courts try to avoid inconsistent judgements in order to preserve reliability and predictability of the law. Therefore, the patient can peacefully await the criminal proceedings' outcome: An acquittal does not affect his civil claim which rests on different, less stringent liability requirements. A criminal conviction on the other hand, will certainly affect his civil suit. Be it that the patient refers to the results of the public prosecutor's investigation and thus decisively eases his task of producing civil evidence; or be it that the physician or the liability insurance behind him, are influenced by the criminal procedure's outcome and admit the claim.

Let me summarize my story:

A patient intending to press civil claims for damages against his physician faces considerable obstacles in terms of evidence and costs. Instead of a investigation by himself or via his attorney, he initiates a criminal investigation and profits from the authorities duty to fully examine the facts. The patient uses public resources to meet his civil ends and later refers in civil court to what has been discovered during the criminal investigation regarding causality and fault.

We can therefore state: A tendency is manifest in the Federal Republic to interfere with and even criminalize medical activities. Because of that a physician faces with increasing frequency the risk of criminal prosecution for his professional activities.

How then can an anaesthetist protect himself against these risks?

From civil claims an anaesthetist can protect himself by taking out a private liability insurance, whereby a coverage for between 2 and 5 million German Marks is recommended. Additionally hospital physicians are usually insured by their hospital's carrier. In the case of hospitals, which do not insure their staff members (public hospitals), the physician has a claim for indemnification against his employer if the patient holds the physician personally liable.

In the case of a criminal procedure only its costs can be covered through an insurance for legal cost. The Association of German Anaesthetists grants its members financial assistance of up to 100.000 German Marks for legal costs above and beyond the-insurable-statutory legal fees.

This was in all brevity an account of the juridical problems caused by anaesthesia accidents and the preventive measures to be taken. So far no mention was made of the difficulties rising in the physician-patient relationship. Please permit me a few remarks in this respect.

The mentioned medical and legal problems are being discussed by laymen and physicians alike with vehemence. By physicians primarily because the legal parameters are capable of shaking the foundation of medical treatment: authority and confidence.

Traditionally these two elements have contributed heavily to the success of medical endeavors. But will therapeutic success not be lost if the physician is forced by extensive information to the patient to cast doubts upon the treatment's success? Will not the sick be left alone with his sufferings if his confidence is shaken? And how can confidence be built up as a sound basis for this relationship if the physician must view the patient as a potential forensic opponent? Are we on the road towards a defensive medicine, afraid of any risk and in the long run preventing medical progress?

To answer this question I think it is helpful to slowly turn away from the typically patriarchal physician-patient relationship and to approach a more partnership-like relationship, one in which the patient participates in the decision making process and bears part of the responsibility. Experience shows that patients are quite willing to take part in this process and to help carry the risk. It goes without saying that the physician always has to follow the ancient rule of "salus aegroti suprema lex" and must, if necessary, accept the forensic risk, that his partnership-like approach overburdens the patient. The hope is justified he will receive judicial understanding in such a case.

One last item should be mentioned. As you have gathered from my explanations, these problem areas are extremely controversial. Both, doctors and lawyers, advocate mutual understanding. Nevertheless, in order to achieve an objective discussion it is mandatory to study facts and processes scientifically. In Germany, however, such academic work encounters an inadequate criminal risk.

Let us assume, for instance, scientific research brings to light a physician's omissions of criminal relevance. The researcher cannot be safeguarded from intervention by the public prosecutor, who in turn may file a criminal investigation against the treating doctor. The researcher will be compelled to make his documents available and testify in court. He can pledge no (so-called) privilege to refuse testimony. This is inadequate. It should be demanded of the lawgiver to grant a scientific privilege in such cases.

I do hope the opening questions and their impact on the development of procedures against anaesthetists in the Federal Republic now becomes somewhat more lucid.

DISCUSSION

A: Discussions about responsability-liability (individual versus joint)

Crul: I would like to bring up two things which may be different between the countries. The first of which is team responsibility and liability. The second is informed consent.

In Holland there is no team liability for the medical profession. Everyone is responsible for his own actions and this is measured in relation to his/her special knowledge and special skills. If something goes wrong the one, who would best be able to deal with that problem, according to his professional knowledge and skills, will be held responsible. If there is damage which cannot be directed to a certain specialist, then all the specialists are charged. All the specialists in the team are sued. The patient can then ask for full repayment of all damages from all the specialists involved, and sometimes even the hospital. This can make it rather profitable for the patient. I understand that there are some decisions by the courts in France, which accept team responsibility. Is this considered a ideal legal situation in cases where there is team responsibility?

Palay-Vincent: During the last twenty years there has often come up a joint liability of surgeons and anaesthetists. Previously, the surgeon was responsible for the whole intervention, and the anaesthetist was only a senior assistant, because there was no contract between the anaesthetist and the patient. The surgeon had to be responsible for the whole team, but when anaesthesia became more independent, we saw (for the first time in 1970) a sole responsibility of the anaesthetist. There is the difficult problem of finding the limits of responsibility of the anaesthetist and to determine the degree of joint action. The difficulty was to delimit the action of each. Now the anaesthetist has his part and the surgeon his part, but that opinion evolved gradually between 1970 and 1980. We have not returned to joint liability because the anaesthetist is put under the surgeon; that is not the problem. Now the courts will consider joint responsibility only because there is in fact a team. You cannot stay passive when you see something done wrong by an other member of the team.

Crul: You mentioned that team members have to supervise each other. In The Netherlands we usually say that we have to warn each other; we have the duty of warning. When you see something done wrong in the other specialty, you have to make a note in your file that you have given a warning. For example, when a tourniquet during operation is blown up too long, there may be some damage to the circulation, or to tissues. Then the anaesthetist has to warn the surgeon after one hour and after one and a half hours that it has been on for that time. If he has not done that or he has not made any notes about doing so, he is also responsible. That is only warning the other team member. In France, however, it is more than only warning, as I understand it.

Palay-Vincent: Yes, I think so. The Farca affair which I spoke about, shows the principle. Here is the problem. The first judgement in Paris found, that only the anaesthetist was responsible. Also the Court of Appeal said that the anaesthetist was solely responsible. The Supreme Court, however, said no. The problem was that the anaesthetist left the private hospital, while the patient had not completely recovered. The Supreme Court said that, because the anaesthetist left, he was at fault. However, the surgeon knew the patient was without assistance, and he left with the anaesthetist. After the Supreme Court it came to the Appeal Court of Versailles where the anaesthetist again was found solely responsible. Just last week we got the new Supreme Court decision which said the surgeon was also responsible, because he knew the situation, and he nevertheles left with the anaesthetist.

René: I think that the Farca case which Mrs. Palay-Vincent described is very important, because it is a decision of the Supreme Court. I have heard the magistrate of the Supreme Court on his analysis and he was very precise.

Lassner: Maybe we should describe what the case was about, because it is important. The patient was a well-known writer, a young man who had an operation on his nose under neurolept analgesia combined with local anaesthesia. The anaesthetist and the surgeon saw the patient at the end of the operation. The patient was sent back to his room. A nurse was in the ward, and some time later she found the patient unconscious. He was resuscitated, but was brain-damaged and died in the end. The fact, that neurolept analgesia can give delayed respiratory depression will be discussed at length at another time during this meeting. The important matter in this case was that quite obviously the accident was linked to the anaesthetic. The anaesthetist was deemed responsible for it, but then came the question of proper supervision of recovery in the hospital, and the fact that both anaesthetist and surgeon knew that no special care was given to the patient. He was in a private room, no special nurse was with him, and the final decision of the Supreme Court reversed the prior decision of the Court of Appeal, which stated that the anaesthetist was solely responsible, on the ground that the anaesthetist and the surgeon left the hospital together. Neither could deny that the other was not present, the surgeon could not say he did not know that the anaesthetist did not take good care of the patient, and they both knew that the patient was not under the care of a special nurse. This was why the Supreme Court considered the surgeon co-responsible for the accident, because he knew about it.

I would like to add one personal experience of this combined responsibility of the surgeon and the anaesthetist for everyone's sake. In 42 years in the practice of anaesthesia I have been sued twice. The first time was when a patient in a private hospital suffered burns on his legs, while undergoing haemorrhoid surgery with a high-frequency coagulator, which was not grounded properly. The claim against me was that possibly the patient had lifted himself from the common ground pad because anaesthesia was not deep enough, and the burn could have occurred by this cause. Since I was able to demonstrate that the surgeon at no time was bothered by the patient's jumping around on the operating table, this was dropped before any lawsuit was ordered against me.

The second time I came into a legal procedure was much later. The case went through various steps for nearly 10 years. An elderly lady underwent endoscopic bladder surgery, a bladder perforation occurred and she died 24 hours later of cardiac failure, probably after insipient peritonitis. The claim against me was, that as I knew the surgeon well, I must have known he was a sick man, and I should have prevented him from operating. The case came into investigation and lasted for 10 years before it was thrown out. The surgeon had cardiac disease, he had undergone cardiac surgery. It was supposed to be my responsibility because I knew he was not fit. You can see that this joint responsibility can be overstretched.

Another case I would like to mention came to court decision quite recently. Mrs. Palay-Vincent has mentioned it. An anaesthetist was condemned for not having properly assisted a patient, who was treated for postoperative ileus, possibly obstruction. The judgement said that it is the duty of the anaesthetist to assist the patient until he recovers full autonomy. Bowel movement was considered part of autonomy. Therefore, the anaesthetist is co-responsible for the patient's care until his bowels move normally, which was two weeks after the operation. To my mind this is an obvious mistake of the court, but it is a mistake we will have to bear for a long time.

Manni: Who is responsible in the theatre for the exact position of the patient on the table? Sometimes an incorrect position can produce troubles for the patient.

Crul: We cannot decide who is responsible; the judge should do that.

Palay-Vincent: The anaesthetist is responsible for positioning of the patient on the operating table, except if the surgeon has certain requirements. In a case in 1978, an arm of a patient was gravely injured because the surgeon asked for a certain position during the whole operation. The court found the surgeon responsible.

Manni: In my opinion, the position of the patient in the theatre is the joint responsibility of the anaesthetist and the surgeon.

Crul: In The Netherlands it is the same as in France, that the prime responsibility for positioning the patient and supervising the places of possible damages from such a position are the responsibility of the anaesthetist. However, if the surgeon insists on a certain position for an operation (even though the anaesthetist has protested against it) the responsibility goes to the surgeon. That is the way it has been dealt with in court in the few cases which occurred in The Netherlands.

Lassner: I saw a case in court, where the patient's arm was injured after brachial plexus block when he was back in bed in his room. The anaesthetist was responsible because it was his anaesthetic, which prevented the patient from repositioning the arm himself. He should have checked the position of the arm of the patient later on.

Wroblewski: It is a bit different in Germany. Generally, the surgeon is responsible for the position of the patient, and liable for any damage. The exception is some anaesthetic requirements, for example, the position of the arm with an infusion in it.

Hargrove: Could I just go back to the question of team responsibility? I think we are fortunate in England that we do not have a team responsibility. It is either the responsibility of the surgeon or the anaesthetist or the nursing staff or the hospital. They are not usually accused together. The only situation where team responsibility comes in is within the specialty. If I am working, as I usually am, with a member of the junior staff, and if I choose to leave that doctor with a patient that is too difficult for him, then the question of negligence in England is judges upon what that doctor should have been able to do with his degree of experience. So, what might be negligent for me is not necessarily negligent for a junior doctor. Under the circumstances, if a patient is damaged by the junior doctor, I carry the responsibility. I would be the one who is sued. From the point of view of team responsibility it is within the specialty, but not in an operating team.

As far as the positioning of the patient is concerned, I think we are very similar to the Germans, in that the positioning of the patient is the responsibility of the surgeon. With the exception, again, of arms which you require for drips of whatever. The responsibility for the placement of the diathermy is a nursing problem, and therefore the nurses or the hospital would be the ones to bear responsibility for that. The responsibility for the tourniquet again is that, whoever applies that tourniquet, is responsible for any damage occurring as a result of the application. But the length of time that the tourniquet is on, is the responsibility of the surgeon. It is considered that the surgeon ought to be able to tell the time, and should be able to know how long the tourniquet has been on.

Crul: Do you also have a responsibility of warning?

Hargrove: We usually do, but there has never been a case yet, when the anaesthetist has been sued because he did not warn the surgeon. Anaesthetists are well looked after from that point of view.

Hallén: Our position on the responsibility for diathermy and positioning is very much the same as what we have just heard, but I would like to return to the question of team responsibility. In Sweden we have nothing of this kind, on the contrary, it has been clearly stated that responsibility is traditionally an individual thing, so that collective responsibility or collective reprisal is basically contradictory to all western judicial tradition. It is, an individual who is responsible, not a community.

Crul: We have the same attitude, that team responsibility might easily lead to individuals hiding behind the team, and that could harm the patient. It would certainly not be the purpose of law to deprive the patient of his rights to have his damage paid for. That is why there is no "team liability". Everyone has that part of the responsibility for which he is supposed to be an expert, and that will be his part of the team responsibility.

Wroblewski: I would like to make two points. The first has to do with responsibility in the case of the patient undergoing nasal surgery under neurolept anaesthesia. We had a similar case to the one you had in France, and the Supreme Court decision was that just by handing over the patient to the nurse, the responsibility went from the anaesthetist to the doctor who is in charge of the ward, so it was a surgical responsibility. If he had stayed in the recovery room, which is under the supervision of the anaesthetist, the responsibility would have been an anaesthetic one. We do not have communal responsibility, we only have individual responsibility.

Barrier: In this decision of the Supreme Court on the Farca case it was not really a team responsibility. The surgeon was condemned because not only did he leave with the anaesthetist, but also because he knew the patient's condition was not good and that the nurse was not a good one, as he had seen the patient in the ward with the anaesthetist before leaving.

Crul: I doubt, whether this decision would have general impact on all other cases of postoperative complication, as this is a very special case, since they went to the patient together and they left the hospital together. That would very rarely be the case. I doubt whether a Supreme Court decision in this case would have an overall effect on all cases of joint responsibility.

René: In France, we say for basic moral responsibility each member of a team is "solitary" and "combined" responsible. But for liability, actually, there is no collective responsibility. There was a case 20 years ago, where the Supreme Court did not conclude to the verdict "liability in solidum", but they were all at fault.

Crul: So they were each responsible but in combination.

Barrier: That is not a true team liability.

Lassner: I would like to tell you about another case and then ask a general question. I was an expert witness in a case which was very similar to the one of the young man operated on the nose, except that the patient was a young lady operated in the belly, but the same type of anaesthetic was given, and the same things happened. Both the surgeon and the anaesthetist had left, and the patient had been sent back to her room. Before leaving they were both speaking to the patient. The husband of the patient was sitting next to her in her room and she was very quiet, and finally was found dead. In the end, there was no doubt, that there was respiratory depression from a rather large dose of phenoperidine. Before the court recessed to deliberate I asked the young colleague who had done the anaesthetic "Do you believe that if you had been this patient, would you have died?". He said "No, obviously not". This ended up in his condemnation in the court. It was not an unfortunate event, it was something directly linked to the lack of vigilance on the part of the anaesthetist.

The second problem I would like to bring up today has to do with a French ruling not concerned with the courts generally, but with medical conduct and with the economic basis of it. In our country all individuals are covered by a system of social security, different from the British one, since it is not run by the state but by a special body called Social Security. It is not financed out of the taxpayers' money but out of the money paid by both employees and employers into this organisation. In the rules of this Social Security, refund of expenses is possible only if the medical procedure has been executed entirely by the same individual. Specifically, to be reimbursed, the doctor must have done the thing himself. If the doctor leaves the scene, as is so frequently seen in anaesthesia, to leave at best a nurse in charge, we cannot possibly say that he has done all the anaesthetic himself, and by signing, that he had done so himself, he is committing an offence. When hospitals bill Social Security for all anaesthetics, regardless of who had administered them, as if they had been administered by doctors, in my mind they are cheating, they are embezzling, and the director of the hospital should be sued and put into prison. Enforcing that rule would be of great help to anaesthetists, because what is permitted in some other countries, that one anaesthetist so-called "supervises" several anaesthetics at the same time, is not so in France. You are personally responsible and should do everything. At the present time the regulations for nurses specify that they cannot give independent anaesthetics, which they nevertheless continue to do, mainly in public hospitals but not in teaching hospitals. Here is something where the law is infringed, because the Social Security system has a lawful basis, but to the best of my knowledge, has never been taken up. Nobody has ever made a claim of this. I would very much wish that anaesthetists as a professional organisation should take up such a case.

Crul: They should make a clear statement on what is acceptable or not, also in the public hospitals. In The Netherlands there have been some disciplinary cases in which anaesthetists had to stop their profession because of cheating like that namely asking for payment for anaesthetics, they had not given themselves.

Lassner: I was an expert witness to a case where the doctor had signed a number of sheets, giving the right to reimbursement. The nurse later put the date on it and the name of the patient. Later it was proven that he had been away from the island where this occurred, for six months, nevertheless his practice was flourishing.

Hargrove: Could I just go back to the original case that you were quoting of the nasal operation? In England that would never have been the responsibility of the surgeon. If the hospital did not have a recovery room, then the hospital is responsible for the death of the patient, because the facilities were not provided for adequate recovery of the patient. I think almost certainly the anaesthetist would have been jointly sued with the hospital for allowing the patient to go back to a room, not even a ward, without being properly recovered. The surgeon would never have been sued; it is not his responsibility to ensure that a patient is adequately recovered. Another difficulty that arises is, where the responsibility ends when you send the patient to the recovery room. We have to ask the nurse each time, whether she is happy to take over the care of a patient. If she is, then it is her responsibility, she has taken on the care. If she is not, then you stay with the patient. We do not have the responsibility to stay with the patient until they are fully conscious, there is no point in having a recovery room if you have that sort of thing, so there is a dual responsibility in the recovery, and the decision to send the patient back to the ward is a nurse's responsibility. If she is uncertain and comes to ask the doctor, then he takes the responsibility. With no recovery facilities in a hospital, they are at fault if a patient goes back to the ward without being fully recovered.

Crul: It is almost the same in The Netherlands.

Lassner: I would like to tell Dr. Hargrove how pleased I am that Brittania rules the waves, because this is strictly a "naval" tradition, and in France, when an officer arrives on the bridge, he always has to stick with the system and call his name and say "I take responsibility", so everybody knows, who is in command.

Wroblewski: It is nearly the same in Germany. There are two sides to it. The moment the patient is given to the ward, the surgeon or the ward is responsible for the patient, yet there can also be the responsibility of the organisation. If, for example, there is no recovery room, only the ward, there could be two people who are sued, the doctor and the organisation (represented by the director), for not providing the right means to take care of the patient.

Roos: I would like to ask Dr. Wroblewski a question. If the surgeon is responsible for the patient as soon as the patient leaves the recovery room, then it seems to me very logical that the surgeon also signs the release form of the recovery room to the ward, because he must accept the responsibility. Otherwise, when the anaesthetist signs the patient out from the recovery room to the ward alone and into the responsibility of the surgeon, you might think that it would be very easy for the anaesthetist to sign out the patient as soon as possible from his own into the surgeon's responsibility without the surgeon being informed and having given consent to do so.

Wroblewski: The responsibility lies not only with the surgeon who did the operation, but also with the doctor who is responsible for the ward. It could be an internal medicine ward or an othopaedic ward; it depends on which ward the patient is coming from. We think, that as long as the patient is in the recovery room he is under the responsibility of the anaesthetist. If the surgeon does not say anything to the effect that he won't take the patient, because he is not happy with the condition, then he takes over the patient and is completely responsible.

Lassner: I think we must consider one difference between Germany and France in this respect. In France, more than half of all surgery is done in private clinics. They are private establishments, run usually on a profit basis, although some are non-profit organisations. In these institutions, there is hardly any provision for real medical coverage and this is one great difference.

Barrier: Midwifery in France is a medical profession, not like in England or Germany. It is a medical profession limited to obstetricians, and midwives are legally allowed to only do normal deliveries independently. For legal reasons, especially on the basis of penal law, the private clinics do not allow the midwives any more to do deliveries. Only a few are continuing. In public hospitals the deliveries are the responsibility of the public service, as Mrs. Palay-Vincent told us. The government, especially the Ministry of Health, does not give money to have doctors do normal deliveries, as it is cheaper to have midwives, because their salaries are lower than the salaries of doctors. The Public Health Service allows the midwives to do deliveries in public hospitals, as they allow nurse-anaesthetists to give anaesthesia under the responsibility of the chief of the department. There is a very big difference between private hospitals and public hospitals in France now.

Hargrove: What is the training of these midwives, are they medically trained or are they trained as nurses?

Barrier: It is somewhere between the two. It is not exactly an academic training, but it is in academic schools, where doctors, dentists and midwives are trained. The midwives, male and female, are specially trained to do obstetrics.

B: Informed consent

Crul: I would like us to move the discussing to the other problem which was mentioned by both Prof. Barrier and Mrs. Palay-Vincent. That is: informed consent. This has become a legal problem now that some countries have extended their informed consent such that they should discuss with the patients everything that could happen to them during anaesthesia. I understand that in Germany it is going to be, or already is, the case that patients even have to be informed of very remote possibilities of damages before anaesthesia, and that may cause unrest and fear in the patient, more than when just a more general approach is used. That is of course also linked with the fact, whether or not the consent has to be in written form. I assume consent in France is only in oral form?

Barrier: Normally it is oral consent, but when doctors think they might have a problem with a patient, sometimes I tell them to get a written letter or to have a witness to what information is given. Sometimes the court requests proof of the consent.

René: The legal opinion in France is, that the time spent by explaining to the patients beforehand about possible accidents is the best protection against later lawsuits. What has not been said, and that I would like to add as a reply to Prof. Crul's request or question is, that up to now there are no recommendations for written consent. And, to the contrary, as has been stated several times, they are useless in court. Therefore, they are not practiced in France, which is much different from what has been happening in Germany where they have become commonplace, as is already a longstanding practice in the United States.

Hargrove: In England there are special cases, in which a necessity of informed consent exists. This is for instance, when a serious complication can occur, be it only in less than 1%. A good example is the possibility of paraplegia after a spondolydesis. Only small risks do not have to be told to patients when it obviously makes them worry. Otherwise signed informed consent forms are necessary. Unless that form has been signed, the anaesthetist and the surgeon are guilty of an assault.

Crul: There has recently been an increasing use of clinical trials, with new drugs, new equipment and new techniques. To what degree do you have to inform patients and ask for their consent to be used for such clinical trials? Do you have any cases in France?

René: There is a difference as to whether the patient himself can possibly profit from the treatment. If so, this is called a trial on a normal individual. Volunteers are not to profit from the treatment, they are treated for the sake of studying something. Only sick people could be treated successfully, otherwise there would not be a treatment.

Lassner: The French Ministry of Health has asked the National Ethical Committee to urgently give its advice on two situations. In the first situation of an eventual benefactory result, the full information is necessary, but then the problem of double blind comes up. In the second situation of an experimental situation on healthy individuals, it has been concluded that a full explanation must be given, and written authorisation must be obtained, either from the subject or from someone in charge of the subject, with particular adjustments for minors or incompetent or unconscious patients. Trials are not permitted on prisoners or on people normally treated by that doctor, because it was felt that then the moral pressure on the patient would be too great to prevent him from refusing.

I would like to add, that we recently had a problem, where one of our colleagues had openly stated that he had tried interosseous injections of large quantities of blood on a individual, who was considered braindead. Nobody had consented to it, obviously not the patient, but also no member of the patient's family had been asked for their consent on the matter. Aside from that, the therapeutic trial was in no way related to the patient's condition, he was simply used as a guinea pig. High-frequency ventilation has also been tried on unconscious patients, who did not actually needed it.

Crul: In The Netherlands we have a very similar rule, that experiments involving additional damage to patients (for example, invasive techniques like putting in Swan-Ganz catheters), can only be done when the patient has signed a written consent to what is going to be done to him aside from the operation involved. Usually - at least this is the opinion of our ethical committees- experiments which only involve extra measurements of parameters taken non-invasively, while sticking to the same rules of anaesthesia, are exempt of the necessity to inform the patient of such extra measurements. Only when the routine procedures of anaesthesia are changed at the same time, informed consent should be given.

Lassner: I would like to make a remark on the question of frequency of the expected event and the necessity to inform about it. I have recently been in charge of an expert testimony on the case of hemiplegia which developed after carotid angiography under general anaesthesia. The radiologist, the neurologist who had prescribed the examination, and the anaesthetist, who had anaesthetized the patient for the examination, had all been accused of negligence, because the patient had not been informed about the risk of hemiplegia. The question then came up of the frequency of hemiplegia after carotid angiography, which is about half a percent. The trial has not ended yet, but the whole matter hinged on the frequency of the complications. Is this a risk which is frequent enough to be included in the information given to the patient? Up to now the only figure existing, to the best of my knowledge, has been around one percent.

Palay-Vincent: Each time there is a decision about lack of information we have the feeling, that when the court cannot establish the causality, it takes the lack of information as a means to compensate the patient.

Hallèn: I would just like to ask a question about experimentation. Suppose you have a seriously ill patient, and you want to experiment with a slightly new or unorthodox drug, you obviously cannot do it in a double blind fashion: how do you handle this? Do you have to go to the ethical committee, in case of an unconscious patient; do you have to ask relatives? You, as a professional,

54

having read the literature, know the patient might probably benefit; how do you handle this?

Palay-Vincent: I take part on a committee at a local hospital in Paris, and we often have the problem of therapeutic trials. Now we always ask for a written consent from the relatives, if the patient is a minor or in a poor state. A few years ago it was difficult to approach a patient or the relatives, today it is not. When it is well explained and some time spent with the family, there seems to be no problem. This is what everyone in the local ethical committee tells us.

René: It is necessary that the trial is ethical, that is well performed. Experimentation must be on a sound scientific basis.

Hargrove: Every hospital in Great Britain has to have its own ethical committee, which usually consists of a lawyer, a churchman, a nurse, and some doctors, who are experienced in clinical trials or research. For a clinical trial of a drug, every patient must sign a separate consent form to say they agree to this treatment. I would like to take up a point made by Dr. Hallén, and that is, that if you have a special case where you feel that it is in the interest of the patient to give a rare drug, we should see no problem with that. It is not referred to the ethical committee, nor do they have a separate consent form. We see this problem constantly in the bone marrow transplantation program, where new drugs are coming up all the time, and we do not involve the patient in that decision. Otherwise we would never know; you cannot do a double blind trial in bone marrow transplantation.

Roos: Do you make any difference between trials in which you use drugs which are already registered in your country and those in which you use drugs which are not yet registered in your country? For instance, if you do clinical trials with fentanyl and droperidol, which are already registered in your country, but you use a slightly different dose, that you usually would use, do you need informed consent from the patient?

Hargrove: If it is a drug that is in constant use, then there is no problem, but if you are comparing that drug with another drug which is not in constant use, then it is a clinical trial and you require the permission of the ethical committee.

Roos: What is your criterion for "in constant use"? Is that being registered?

Hargrove: It has to be in the British Pharmacopoeia, and it would have to be in use such, that a normal doctor would prescribe it for the treatment of that patient. We do not agree with drugs being given to patients, which do not contribute towards their treatment. With volunteers it is different, but if it is a patient you are using, it is very important that you should be able to say

"This drug, we think, will contribute towards the patient's treatment". If it does not, you should not be using it; it would not get through the ethical committee.

Roos: If you think that a drug would contribute to a patient's well-being but it is not registered, you need informed consent, and if it is registered, you do not?

Hargrove: That is right.

Roos: Then it is the same as in The Netherlands.

Barrier: What is the rule in England for the unusual indication of a registered drug, a well-known nationally registered drug with a new indication?

Hargrove: You are thinking of something like putting opiates into the extradural space. You would have to get informed consent and it would have to go to the ethical committee.

Lassner: In France, trials have to be approved by the Minister of Health. There are a certain number of rules for them, and informed consent is part of it. However, no one can conduct an organised trial without applying for the permission to do so and having proper insurance coverage.

Crul: I would like to go on to something else which is evolving now in the different countries. That is, that we are all trying to attain proper Standards of Care. This is being made more easy and more flexible, by standards set by the decisions of the law courts and by recommendations by the Ministry of Health. It also avoids the necessity to make special laws for it. We have been hearing that their use is increasing in France as is the case in The Netherlands, and it turns out that the recommendations by the Ministry of Health work just as effectively as laws or legal decisions. They work more easily, because they can be presented much more quickly, yet they have almost the same civil effect. What do, particularly the lawyers among us, think about the shift from laws to recommendations by the Ministries? Do you think it is a good change or are you at all reluctant to take these recommendations from the Ministry of Health or other organs into your armamentarium to defend cases or to accuse defendants?

Palay-Vincent: I think, that when we defend a practitioner it is very important to have such recommendations. For instance, with the recommendation of 1974 for a recovery room I had solid arguments to defend a practitioner and demonstrate that it was the hospital's responsibility.

Wroblewski: I think it is interesting because there is a difference between the two countries. In Germany we do not have the recommendations by the Ministry of Health at all, we only have recommendations by the professional body of anaesthetists. These recommendations do have meaning in court, but the professional body is very restrictive in their recommendations, because they can be used in court. We have Supreme Court opinions, which have a very great influence on standards of care in hospitals. For example, there is a Supreme Court opinion with regard to using ECG during induction. If you do not use it and an accident happens, it does not look good for him.

Crul: Does the Supreme Court also go by the advice of an expert witness?

Wroblewski: Yes, of course they depend strongly on the expert witness.

Crul: The expert witness, then, is a very important person in this respect.

Lassner: I would like to demonstrate why recommendations by the Ministry and the law do not have the same importance. When we came up with the recommendation for the recovery room in 1974, most private nursing homes in France achieved at least a resemblance of something like a recovery room, to be prepared for a possible lawsuit. Ten years later, nearly two-thirds of the public hospitals, except the university teaching hospitals, did not have a recovery room because they are state-dependent. No financial means had been available, because it was not a law, just a recommendation, and since they insure themselves, they thought it would make a difference in money. Therefore, they did not do it. If it had been a law, the state would have had to provide the necessary money to comply. With a recommendation it does not. This is the main difference between recommendation and law: money.

Crul: In Holland we have two types of law, the very solid and widely discussed ones and what we call "een maatregel van bestuur", a kind of decree, which is made by the minister, but which does not have to go through all the discussions and approvals of both the chambers of the parliament.

Wroblewski: "Verordnung" in Germany.

Roos: Every law which is made, has to be followed by an administrative rule, and then there are some administrative rules without any law beforehand, which are a sort of decrees for public interest.

Lassner: Also in our country a law has to be followed by a "decrée d'application", and if not added, nothing will happen.

Crul: These decrees are increasing in number, but they still take a long time to come into action. We are therefore more inclined to ask the Ministry of Health to support our suggestions and approve of them, and consequently sending them out to all the hospitals. These are used often and readily by the law courts as a kind of standard of care accepted by the Ministry of Health and by the professional group. Would that be possible in France too? It is more or less your "regulations by the Minister of Health".

Barrier: As Professor Lassner said, these regulations are not law, but on the basis of these regulations, private doctors were condemned.

Palay-Vincent: I think these regulations are really important now. They are not really law as such, but the court can appreciate the situation better when taking them into consideration.

Wroblewski: It is interesting that in Germany we do not have a State influence on the meaning of laws or administrative rules in the health sector. Whatever you do as a medical doctor is up to self-organised professional bodies in the various areas. The only control is by the judiciary, so it is not the state who says what you have to do, they say that what you do is up to the professional body, and you have to set your own standards. Whether those standards are acceptable, can only be proven by the individual case in front of court, but when administrative rules, no laws exist, it is just an individual case.

Crul: Yes, that is quite different.

Hargrove: We do not have a Ministry of Health, we have a Department of Health and Social Security, it is just another name. They lay down specific regulations, for instance, on the design of hospital buildings. Any new hospital which is being designed, must incorporate, say, a gas pipeline system, a recovery room, or so many operating theatres per number of patients. There are many regulations which are laid down and which can be used in court, either against the doctors or against the health authority. The Department of Health in England is divided into 14 different Health Authorities, which cover the country, and it is up to the Health Authorities to implement the regulations. It comes down to hospital and individual doctor level when they issue what they call "hazard warnings". If a piece of equipment is shown to be harzardous or dangerous to the patient, they will issue a hazard warning note that goes to every hospital. It is up to every hospital to issue that note to every doctor concerned, and it is up to every doctor to ensure that that piece of equipment is taken out of service. Those hazard warnings come from the Department of Health like confetti. They constantly pour in. I had ten on my desk in one day, involving things like dangerous carpets, incubators, warming pads, and monitoring equipment. They are constantly pouring into the hospitals. These hazard warnings are quoted in law; they do not loose legal impact simply by being so numerous. The hazard warning, for instance, on pipelines, was issued about four years before our pipeline disaster occurred at Westminster, and it was quoted extensively.

Crul: The use of these hazard warnings is another way of approaching the increase in the standards of care.

Lassner: In 1979 we were notified about the implementation of a type of hospitals building, prefabricated buildings, already ordered by the Minister of Health, in 12 individual design examples, but which did not include any anaesthetic department or room. I went to see the Minister of Health to complain officially as a representative of the French Anaesthetists about the contracts given to the building company for 12 hospitals without anaesthetic facilities. He told me it could not be changed, and that the plans had been made in 1930!

Crul: We have heard the basic principles of legal liability laws in the different countries, and we have discussed the problems emerging from such basic principles. Now we will devote our attention to the facts, to liability cases, and their probable causes and the main strong points of the legal aspects, in the different countries contributing to this workshop.

AWARENESS - A MEDICO-LEGAL PROBLEM

R.L. Hargrove

A patient signing a consent form and agreeing to have an operation performed under general anaesthesia expects to be unconscious and free from pain or unpleasant sensation during the surgical procedure. He or she does not anticipate hearing a surgeon and assistant conversing while they work. Yet, since the advent of muscle relaxant drugs and their introduction to anaesthetic practice in the 1940's the possibility of a paralysed patient remaing awake has become a reality, fortunately a very uncommon experience but one that in recent years is seemingly on the increase. A number of cases have been reported from time to time, but for the past fifteen years the Medical Defence Union has been receiving an average of four or five cases per year.

In 1985, a patient in Wigan sued her anaesthetist because she was awake during a Caesarian section. The facts of the case were very much in her favour so that damages in excess of £ 13.000 were awarded to her and the whole affair attracted considerable publicity. As a result a whole series of claims were made by patients that they too had been awake during various surgical procedures. Public realisation of a potential hazard of a medical procedure frequently leads to an increase in claims against doctors and not all the claims are related to events in recent years. A number will inevitably be made for events that occurred many years, perhaps even decades, previously. Following the Wigan case, claims of awareness during general anaesthesia have been made for events that occurred as long ago as 1979. The Statute of Limitations in theory bars a plaintiff from making a first claim for events that occurred more than three years previously, but in practice it is not difficult for this limitation to be overcome.

An anaesthetist would do well to reflect that a patient who claims to have been awake during an operation is very likely to be correct.

Some such claims are undoubtedly spurious, while others may be based upon a hazy recollection of immediate post anaesthetic dreams or other para-operative phenomena. Most claims, particularly those which detail severe pain or discomfort, the inability to breath or awareness of the noise of their surroundings, carry the ring of truth. Frequently, patients subsequent complaints and recollection of events in the operating theatre can be verified in detail, by those who were present at the time.

An increase in number of genuine claims by patients of awareness during general anaesthesia very probably bears some relationship to the current anaesthetic practice of supplementing nitrous-oxide and oxygen anaesthesia with intravenous narcotic analgesic drugs rather than inhalational agents. While adequate doses of narcotic analgesics usually ensure that a patient is pain free, they do not offer a certainty that a patient will be unaware, least of all when the ratio of oxygen to nitrous-oxide is more than 30%.

It is too frequently assumed that awareness during general anaesthesia is restricted to obstetric anaesthetic practice. Although such cases figure prominently in litigation they account for only 28% of all the cases of awareness reported to the Medical Defence Union. Anaesthesia for general surgical procedures accounted for 31% of cases and a further 18% involved patients undergoing gynaecological procedures. There were 11% of cases associated with orthopaedic operations and the remaining 12% of cases were associated with dental, ENT and ophthalmological operations. It is clear that most cases of reported awareness occurred in situations where there was no requirement for a minimal level of analgesia.

Reasons For Awareness During General Anaesthesia
The cases reported to the Medical Defence Union can be classified according to the probable reason for the awake state.

1. Faulty anaesthetic technique
The majority of cases (70%) fall into this category and most of these are, where the anaesthetist has relied upon the nitrous-oxide:oxygen:narcotic sequence to ensure unconsciousness. This may result in awareness in a proportion of cases. Where a volatile agent has been used it has either been in too small a concentration or has only been used intermittently during the anaesthetic. In Caesarian section cases it seems common practice to give a small dose of thiopentone (3.5 mg per kg) or methohexitone (1 mg per kg) followed by succinylcholine. After intubation the patient is ventilated with a 50-50 mixture of nitrous-oxide and oxygen until the baby is delivered. Frequently, after delivery, if a narcotic is given it is in a very small dose and no allowance is made for the time it takes for an intravenous dose to act. There seems to be a reluctance, on the part of junior anaesthetists in particular, to use a volatile supplement (e.g. 0.5% halothane) in the period between induction of anaesthesia and delivery of the baby. The greatest risk

of awareness occurs in this period. There is no good evidence to show that babies born to mothers having only nitrous oxide and oxygen are in a better condition than those where the mother has had a volatile agent given as part of the technique. Indeed, it is possible that if the mother is awake during the operation the result of the increased catecholamine output could easily result in delivery of a baby who is in a worse rather than a better state. Where the Caesarian section is being performed for severe foetal distress, some anaesthetists might feel that very light anaesthesia is justified but again, there is no good evidence to show such a technique is to the advantage of the baby or the mother. If the anaesthetist really believes that very light anaesthesia is justified then he must ensure that the patient is fully acquainted with the possibility of being aware. If he does not inform the patient of this possibility, and the patient subsequently sues, it makes it much more difficult to defend him on a charge of negligence.

Another group of patients who are at risk from a faulty technique are those admitted as day cases. They are usually unpremedicated and given small doses of a short acting induction agent, sometimes followed by a relaxant. Unless great care is taken in ventilating these patients with a gas mixture that ensures unconsciousness, awareness will occur in a number of cases. There is a tendancy to paralyse intubate and ventilate patients when the indication for such a technique does not exist. Patients having operations requiring little or no relaxation, e.g. on the limbs, seldom require to be paralysed and ventilated, but may well need a volatile or other supplement to maintain reflex inactivity. Fewer orthopedic cases would come to litigation if this fact was appreciated. Patients have also been awake due to the inattention of the anaesthetist or his absence from the operating theatre altogether. Such episodes are unforgiveable and indefensible.

Finally, the difficult intubation is a common cause of temporary awareness. If the dose of induction agent is small and difficulties arise in intubating the patient there is a tendency to give the patient more relaxant without giving an additional dose of the induction agent. This particularly applies to Caesarian sections. Such a technique will evitably result in the patient being aware of the attempted intubation and there have been several graphic accounts of what it feels like to have a laryngoscopy and attempted intubation while awake and paralysed.

2. Failure to check apparatus

Twenty percent of cases of awareness are the direct result of the anaesthetist failing to check his anaesthetic apparatus. Difficulties arise when the connection between the anaesthetic machine and the ventilator is loose or completely disconnected. Under certain circumstances the patient can then be ventilated with room air alone and is wide awake and in pain. It is surprising that the anaesthetist involved does not notice the rising blood pressure and pulse rate or the sweating, lachrymating patient.

In some cases the emergency oxygen control was left on and the inflating gases were diluted to the extent that the patient could not possibly be unconscious. Checking of the apparatus before attaching the patient to the ventilator would have overcome these difficulties.

Cases of awareness have arisen as a result of the vaporizer not being correctly locked on the back bar of the anaesthetic machine. In other cases flexible connections to the vaporizer have become detached through back pressure or failure to check the security of the tapered fittings. Disconnections, partial or complete, account for other cases in this section and the message must be that checking of the anaesthetic apparatus before every case is esssential.

3. Genuine apparatus failure

Where part of the anaesthetic apparatus fails, and this could not have been detected by a diligent anaesthetist using the normal methods of testing prior to the start of the anaesthetic, then this can be considered a genuine apparatus failure. Included under this heading would be vaporizers which given concentrations of vapour well below that indicated by the dial setting. Ventilators have been known to malfunction and allow the patient to be ventilated with low concentrations of nitrous-oxide. Here again an anaesthetist could not be expected to detect the fault in the apparatus though he should perhaps be able to recognise the signs of light anaesthesia. From the medico-legal point of view the manufacturers of faulty apparatus would usually be expected to contribute to any damages awarded in such a case.

4. Spurious claims

Publicity surrounding cases of awareness undoubtedly generates an attitude in some members of the general public that money can be obtained by merely stating that awareness has taken place. This, in the eyes of the law, is insufficient to constitute a case of negligence against the anaesthetist. When these patients are asked for more details of the awareness it soon becomes evident that such an event did not take place and the claim is entirely spurious. These cases can be contested and are often withdrawn before they reach the courts. Two and a half percent of cases fall into this category.

5. Justified risks

Where a patient is desperately ill and is in a life threatening situation on the operating table, it is not unreasonable for the anaesthetitst to keep the patient very lightly anaesthetised during this critical phase of the operation. Occasionally, the patient will recall events during the period of light anaesthesia but is is unusual for the patient to sue the anaesthetist - they are usually very grateful for all the efforts that have been made to save their lives. Sometimes the patient will not take that attitude and feels that money is needed to compensate them for the discomfort of the situation. This would be a case where the M.D.U. would fight vigorously on behalf of the anaesthetist because there is no evidence of negligence. Lastly there will be the occasional patient who complains of awareness where the anaesthetic technique appears to be flawless. The complaint would appear to be genuine and the anaesthetic records impeccable, so it is difficult in these cases to know exactly what happened. It could have been a genuine apparatus failure which remained undetected or it could have been that the anaesthetist's records were either not accurate or filled in after the event occurred. The patients in this group only constitute 2.5% of the total number of cases of awareness.

Seniority of anaesthetist involved

Sixty-three percent of cases involved a member of the junior staff and the remaining 37% were cases anaesthetised by consultants. Many of the junior staff said that they were only carrying out the instructions of their consultants in using a particular technique. This applied especially to Caesarian sections. In some cases a specified technique has been written down and such a document can often be shown to outline a technique, that will undoubtedly result in awareness in a proportion of cases. In this situation the anaesthetist who has laid down the technique to be followed, must bear the blame for errors of the junior staff.

It is distressing to find that more than a third of cases are the responsibility of anaesthetists of consultant grade i.e. people with qualifications and experience who should be able to detect signs of awareness in their patients.

It may be excusable for an S.H.O. in the first six months of his job to have a problem with awareness but there is seldom any reason for a consultant to find himself in the same position.

The claim by the patient

The patient may complain while in hospital, but the first notification that an anaesthetist usually gets is a letter from a solicitor. Later a Written Statement of Claim which set out the details of the complaint and the allegations of negligence may be received. Prompt counselling and reassurance by the anaesthetist concerned, while the patient is in hospital, and as soon as possible after the event, offer the best chance of avoiding a claim at a later stage. If this fails to work and the anaesthetist receives a solicitor's letter, he should then report the whole matter to his defence society at once. The defence society will refer his case to an anaesthetic advisor, who will be primarily interested in attempting to establish whether or not the claim is genuine. There may be good evidence of awareness such as a description of the intubation, presence of auditory sensation (in particular details of conversation in the operating theatre), a feeling of paralysis and the inability to communicate with those present in the operating theatre. The patient may also be able to describe the various stages of the operation and the actions of the anaesthetist, e.g. retracting the eyelids to look at the pupil. Finally, there is often a description of pain. All this evidence would come from the patient and is not always available in detail when the anaesthetic advisor first assesses the case. It must be accepted that a patient can, in exceptional circumstances, obtain most of his "evidence" to make a claim from a variety of sources, but in genuine cases some of the facts are difficult to dispute. A genuine claim is usually supported by evidence from the details of the actual anaesthetic, but only when such details are readily available. The absence of anaesthetic records makes defence of a claim, genuine or false, very difficult. A contemporaneous anaesthetic chart is of the greatest value. It may record evidence very suggestive of inadequate anaesthesia. It may display the choice and use of drugs, and the patient's response to them at surgical intervention, in terms of blood pressure, pulse rate and autonomic parameters that are not unlikely to be associated with a conscious patient. It is the anaesthetic advisor's task to match the patient's allegations with the anaesthetist's account and the anaesthetic charts. A defence in court can only be made when there is clear evidence against the claim. Lack of such evidence will almost certainly lead a judge to sentence in favour of the patient. When a claim cannot be defended or when it appears to be genuine, the defence society concerned will settle the case on behalf of the anaesthetist. If it can be shown that there was a failure in the equipment used by the anaesthetist and that this failure could not be anticipated or easily detected by the anaesthetist, then the manufacturers of the equipment would be expected to contribute at least in part of the settlement.

Prevention

If we are to prevent an increase in the number of cases of awareness, anaesthetists must be even more meticulous in their techniques. Whilst it is not possible to provide a recipe for unconsciousness in every case, adherence to certain principles will ensure that the incidence of awareness is considerably reduced.

These principles should include:
a. the checking of all apparatus both in the anaesthetic room and the operating theatre before the start of every operating list and if necessary before each case;
b. the use of adequate premedication with perhaps a greater use of amnesic drugs;
c. the administration of proper doses of induction agents. The 'sleep dose' should not be thought of as the upper limit, particularly in fit young individuals. Particular attention should be paid to the dosage of the ultrashort acting induction agents;
d. consider the use of a volatile agent as part of all those techniques where the patient is to be paralysed and ventilated. Reliance should not be placed on the nitrous oxide:oxygen:narcotic sequence alone as a mean of securing unconsciousness;
e. where the intubation is difficult, ensure that further doses of induction agent are given when supplements of the relaxant are also being given;
f. await the full reversal of all paralysing drugs before turning off the nitrous oxide. Many patients are aware of the events towards the end of an operation;
g. inform all patients having a Caesarian section of the possibility of awareness and the reasons behind it. Make sure that such a warning is entered on the anaesthetic record.
h. it has been suggested that the use of earplugs on patients would help to

cut down the auditory input. This is only acceptable provided all other efforts to prevent awareness are made at the same time;
i. ensure that all apparatus is under a service contract and that servicing visits are made at the correct intervals.

As with all other aspects of anaesthesia, success can only be assured by correct assessment and counseling of the patients pre-operatively, the use of equipment which has been shown to be without fault, a meticulous technique and a vigilant attitude throughout the operation and into the postoperative period. It is to be hoped that with this attitude on the part of all anaesthetists, awareness will be eliminated as an entity in the future.

DELAYED RESPIRATORY EFFECTS OF THE ADMINISTRATION OF THE NEW MORPHINOMIMETICS

F. Marchetti

1. Introduction

Respiratory depression is the most common and dangerous side effects of opioids especially when it occurs unpredictibly and delayed. Late respiratory depression occurs with the newest highly potent analgesics. It is interesting to look into the published data for a better understanding of this phenomenon.
In several countries, two new morphinomimetics are already on the market: sufentanil and alfentanil. The purpose of this presentation is to consider physicochemical and pharmacokinetic parameters of these new drugs in order to evaluate the possibilities of occurrence of these accidents.

2. Delayed respiratory depressions after use of fentanyl

2.1 Medical data already published

From 1976 through 1983 many articles were published about this subject. Becker (1976) noted the occurrence of biphasic respiratory depression, when either fentanyl alone or innovar (fentanyl + droperidol) were used as a supplement to nitrous oxide anaesthesia.
Adams and Pybus (1978) observed delayed respiratory depression in three patients after apparent recovery. They were treated successfully with naloxone. Mac Quay et al. (1978) measuring fentanyl plasma concentrations reported secondary peaks several hours after surgery. Lehman et al. (1982) measuring the fentanyl plasma concentration as well as the blood gases over a long period (8 hours) after extubation, noted a great variability in the fentanyl plasma concentrations between 0.2 and 6.8 ng/ml. The threshold concentrations for spontaneous ventilation are between 1 and 2 ng/ml, according to Stansky and Hug (1982). However Lehman et al. never observed clinical signs of respiratory depressions, and correlation between $P_a CO_2$ and fentanyl plasma concentrations was not present.
Their conclusions confirm the importance of the lack of environmental stimuli in the occurrence of postoperative depression.

67

Stoeckel et al. (1982) trying to correlate plasma fentanyl concentrations with respiratory depression, studied in healthy volunteers plasma levels and CO_2 response curves after bolus injections of fentanyl 0.5 mg. This is the only study which corroborates the hypothesis of correlation between respiratory depression and secondary plasma peaks. Nillson and Rosberg (1982) published 3 other similar cases. Cartwright et al. (1983) studied 4 groups of patients with two doses of fentanyl 10 mcg/kg or 25 mcg/kg and 2 types of P_aCO^2 response curves. One sub-group was ventilated with P_aCO_2 between 38 and 45 torr and the other group between 20-25 torr. Respiratory depressions only occurred in the group with high doses of fentanyl and in the sub-group with hyperventilation.

These studies show that secondary fentanyl peaks exist and their occurrences are unpredictible and delayed. In certain circumstances these rebounds are accompanied by respiratory depressions. Two factors seem to increase this phenomenon: high doses of fentanyl and hypocapnia following mechanical hyperventilation.

2.2 Hypothesis of the possible explanation of this phenomenon

Enterosystemic recirculation:
Stoeckel et al. (1982) gave the first explanation: in animals fentanyl is secreted by the stomach and intestinal reabsorption into the enterohepatic system explains the rebound rise of the plasma concentration. In human beings the magnitude of the hepatic first-pass effect means that this is only part of the explanation (Lehman et al., 1982).

Redistribution from the tissues:
The more likely explanation would be the redistribution from the deep compartments. They account for the large volume of distribution of fentanyl. In fact, fentanyl is stocked in the deep compartments, composed of muscles and fat, and redistribution occurs during the recovery after the end of the operation. The end of paralysis and mobilisation of the patients speeds up this effect.
Lehman (1982) observed an increase in fentanyl plasma concentration after the removal of a tourniquet on the thigh.

Protein binding and pH variations:
Another factor could facilitate the rebound rise of fentanyl plasma concentration. The change in pH increases the free fraction of the drug, which is the active part. This increase combined with acidosis may cause the remorphinisation phenomenon.

2.3 Conclusion

The plasmatic rebounds are more likely to be explained by the redistribution from the deep compartment than by enterosystemic absorption after secretion in the stomach.
In the recovery period all physiological parameters are modified. The passage of fentanyl from the deep towards the central compartment is facilitated by the mobilisation of the patients, the change in hemodynamic and pH parameters. The clinical respiratory depression is increased by hypocapnia.

3. Physicochemical and pharmacokinetic parameters of the new opioids sufentanil and alfentanil

If we consider the pharmacokinetic properties of these new drugs, the differences are especially related to smaller volume of distribution and shorter terminal half-life (table 1).

TABLE 1: Pharmacocinetic parameters of new opioids

	phenoperidine	fentanyl	alfentanil	sufentanil
clearance ml/min/kg	23,00	12,00	5,00	10,00
Vd ss l/kg	5,70	4,20	0,60	2,30
Beta-halflife (h)	3,20	3,70	1,50	2,70

3.1 Sufentanil

The volume of distribution of sufentanil is 2.3 l/kg to 3 l/kg. It is below the value for fentanyl but not so much that the possibility of secondary peaks can be neglected. But the first results of pharmacokinetic studies have shown that they are unfrequent and smaller than after the use of fentanyl.

3.2 Alfentanil

Alfentanil is an original drug in its range, because its pharmacokinetic profile linked so well to its physicochemical characteristics.
Its low Pka (6.5) causes a large unionized part of the drug at normal pH, which contains the diffusible and active part of the drug (table 2).

TABLE 2: Correlation between Pka and non-ionised fractions of the new opiods in plasma

	phenoperidine	fentanyl	alfentanil	sufentanil
Pka	8,01	8,40	6,50	8,00
% non-ionised	20,30	8,50	88,80	20,30

In addition, the partition coefficient expressed in log P accounts for a relatively low lipid solubility. The association of these parameters with the high affinity for the plasmatic proteins explains its small volume of distribution, producing the short elimination half-life and therefore the low risk of recirculation.
Unfortunately, some respiratory depressions were also described with these 2 new drugs. Are these events significant? Can they be predicted?

4. Respiratory depressions after use of sufentanil and alfentanil

4.1 Sufentanil

Sufentanil was used in more than 4 million hours of anaesthesia all over the world, and, only three cases of respiratory depression were published. Only one seemed correlated with an elevated sufentanil level. This clinical report by Wiggun et al. (1986) concerns a patient with a chronic renal failure during the insertion of a peritoneal dialysis catheter (table 3).

TABLE 3 :	Clinical report (Wiggum et al 1985)
1 Patient	68 y, 80 kg
	Chronic renal failure
Medication:	Quinidine 300 mg
Total dose of sufentanil:	120 mcg
Fully awake: 2 apnoeas in the first hour without muscle rigidity	
Naloxone 0,4 mg:	no improvement

The sufentanil levels were determined using a gas chromatographic method described by Weldon et al. (1986). A polemic about the viability of this method was going on in Anesthesiology with the replies of Heykants et al., Griffiths and Avram et al. (1986). The conclusions are that this paper is questionable and that the high sufentanil level detected was largely overestimated by the presence of quinidine or one of its metabolites.
The two other cases were published, one by Goldberg et al. (1986) and the second by Chang et al. (1986) (table 4).

TABLE 4:	Clinical report (sufentanyl)
2 Patients	35-36 y, 75-85 kg
Duration of operation:	2,5 h.
Total dose:	225-300 mcg
Clear/awake: thoracic muscle stiffness, apnoea 20 min. after the end of the operation.	

These patients were comparable in weight, age and duration of surgery. Both presented after clear alertness and adequate ventilation for the first 20 minutes, a sudden respiratory arrest with rigidity. In the first case, the patient was ventilated during the period of unsatisfactory ventilation (table 4). In the second case, naloxone was successfully used. The explanation of these events is for Hilberman and Hyer (1986) a sufentanil overdose. These authors use the well known formular from Goodman and Gilman (1981) to calculate the right dose:

loading dose = target concentration x volume of distribution
maintenance dose = target concentration x clearance.

72

On table 5, the administrated doses compared to the calculated doses are shown for both patients. Goldberg accepted Hilberman's explanation.

TABLE 5: Recommended doses of orioids for steady analgesia

Total dose calculated for patient of Goldberg:	134 mcg
Total dose administered:	300 mcg
Total dose calculated for patient of Chang:	152 mcg
Total dose administered:	225 mcg

4.2 Alfentanil

Alfentanil was used in more than 1 million hours, and 7 cases of respiratory depression were observed and 3 of them published: one by Lamarche et al. (1984) and two by Sebel et al. (1984).
In table 6 the clinical parameters are presented.

TABLE 6: **Clinical reports (alfentanil)**

7 Patients	1 of 72 y, 6 of approx. 45 y
	65-89 kg
Duration of surgery:	1-3 h.
Total dose:	125-570 mcg/kg
Fully awake.	
Apnoea:	20 min. after the end of surgery

All the patients were premedicated with a benzodiazepine which could prolonge the duration of action. Alfentanil was used by infusion during more than one hour. One dose was very high (570 mcg/kg). One patient was old and it is well known that the terminal half-life is longer in elderly patient. The apnea occurred 20 minutes after the end of surgery and was antagonized by just one dose of naloxone.
The use of alfentanil by infusion produces a change in the pharmacokinetics. Reitz (1986) noted a decrease of clearance and an increase of the terminal half-life. Bower and Hull (1982) related this phenomenon to the individual variability of the protein binding with alpha 1 glyco-protein acid and to the reduction of hepatic blood flow according to the long duration of surgery. For

Stansky and Hug (1982) the time to obtain satisfactory ventilation after an infusion of opioids is linked to the target concentration at the steady state. The higher it is, the longer spontaneous ventilation will be postponed.

CONCLUSION

It is evident that all the patients who have received opioids need respiratory attention for a certain period during the recovery depending on the dose and the duration of infusion. Anesthesiologists know very well that respiratory depression by opioids is due to an inadequate response of the respiratory centers to CO_2: Noxious stimuli maintain apparently satisfactory ventilation. However, in the quietness of the recovery room the patient falls asleep again and stop breathing.

Up till now, in the cases of both alfentanil and sufentanil no late rebound rises of the plasma levels after operation were observed.

The delayed respiratory depression sometimes caused by the new morphinomimetics extends the time of legal responsability of the anaesthetists' way beyond the time of actual anaesthesia and even up till 24 hours after the end of operation. If they cannot provide adequate supervision themselves, they are legally obliged to transfer this responsability to properly trained and authorized (para)medical personnel. This personnel should at all times be equiped with tools to detect and subsequently combat respiratory depression.

Records of respiratory functions of the patient should be maintained during these 24 hours.

MEDICO-LEGAL CONSEQUENCES DERIVING FROM INQUIRIES ON THE INCIDENCE OF ANAESTHETIC MISHAPS

J. Lassner

1. Recent European Inquiries on anaesthetic mis. aps

The scientific session of the European Academy of Anaesthesiology in 1982 dealt with Mortality in Anaesthesia (Vol. 3 of the Academy's Proceedings, published by Springer Verlag, Berlin, 1983). On that occasion, F. Hatton et al. presented a first account (p. 25-38) of a study conducted in France. In parallel, J.N. Lunn gave a first account of a study then ongoing in the U.K. (p. 19-24). Both have since been published. An English language version of the French study originally published in "Annales Francaises d'anesthésie et de rénamimation", (Vol. 2, 5, 1983) has appeared in the Canadian Journal of Anaesthesia. The first study in the U.K. has been followed recently by a new one, presently available from the Nuffield Provincial Hospitals Trust, 3 Prince Albert Road, London: "The Report of a confidential Enquiry into Peri-operative Deaths", prepared by N. Buck, H.B. Devlin and J.N. Lunn.

Only the French study was prospective. One thirteenth of all anaesthetics administered during a given year (nearly 200.000 cases) were closely monitored. The geographical and chronological distribution of the cases had been chosen so as to make the sample appropriate for statistical evaluation on a nation-wide basis. In connection, it should be noted that in France surgery is performed, both in public hospitals and in private institutions called "cliniques", with nearly equal numbers of operations per year in the two categories.

2. Legal follow-up

In the volume of Proceedings mentioned above, there is a study by J. Montagne (p. 104-106) on the medico-legal consequences of anaesthetic mishaps in France. Anybody concerned by such an event can either sue for damages in a civilian court or try to initate criminal proceedings by alleging unlawful conduct on the part of one or several doctors. The administrative courts are competent for any alleged damage resulting from the inadequacies of public hospitals. While civic and administrative claims must be filed by lawyers and are costly, anybody may write a letter to the public prosecutor to request an inquiry for an alleged breach of the law. Even if no legal action is finally taken, the doctor concerned by an official inquiry, initially conducted by police officers and often given publicity in the press, suffers great hardship.

For financial reasons, the request for a penal inquiry is chosen by those who consider themselves victims of malpractice in preference to the two other means. Nearly two thirds of all actions are initiated in this way. While such actions have been increasing year after year, their total does not presently exceed about one hundred per year for cases filed against anaesthetists. Only about one quarter of the cases end with a condemnation of the accused. These figures are derived from the records of insurance companies and do not include the inquiries which are not followed by court proceedings. The statistics of the Ministry of Justice do not single out the cases involving anaesthetists.

3. Numerical results and their possible consequencies

Among the 200.000 cases included in the French study, life threatening or permanent damage accidents occurred in 268 cases, 1,35% of the total. This figure concerns only accidents connected with or attributed to anaesthesia. Death or coma immediately following the anaesthetic and attributed to it occurred within the first 24 hours after the operation in 83 cases or 0,42%.

As indicated before, the size of the sample (exactly 198.103 cases) was 1/13th of the number of anaesthetics performed in one year in France. By multiplying the observed number of deaths attributed to anaesthesia in the sample, 83, by 13, an annual total of 1.079 anaesthetic deaths would have to be presumed. The mortality rate for anaesthesia in this study is much higher than those given in other recent inquiries, generally retrospective. The latter like the UK report, cover not only the first postoperative day (as in the French study) but a full week. Before concluding that there is a greater risk for the practice of anaesthesia in France than in the UK or elsewhere, one would have to make sure that the retrospective studies are really comprehensive.

In any case it is evident from these considerations that it would be of considerable public interest to initiate comparative inquiries. The European Academy could play a useful role in preparing such studies, involving several European countries.

The number of anaesthetic deaths likely to have occurred is ten times higher than the number of court proceedings involving anaesthetists. Obviously, an anaesthetic-related death does not necessarily mean a death due to anaesthetic malpractice. Still, it should be recalled that most published studies involve human error in more than two thirds of all cases.

If one were to include life-threatening accidents and those resulting in permanent damage, the figures would be much higher: 268 x 13 = 3.484. Most of the time such accidents remain unknown to the patient. On the other hand, some forms of permanent damage, such as broken teeth, are often the basis for claims.

Looking for an upper limit for possible claims, one could add up the two categories, death and coma, for instance one half of life-threatening complications or permanent damage, 1.079 + 3.484/2 = 2.821 cases out of 3.6 million anaesthetics.

The potential number of claims is rather frightening! It should be recalled that mishap does not mean fault, but let us nevertheless look more closely into means of reducing the risk both to patients and to anaesthetists.

4. Circumstances of accidents

In the French study, a number of elements relating to the accidents and deaths have been considered. While the comparison of rates between various types of institutions may be useful as a yardstick for the quality of care, the former are strongly influenced by patients selection. Because of the well-known increase in death rate according to the age of the patients, only samples with reasonably similar composition with respect to age distribution should be compared. The same holds true for social stratification.

The vexed question of differences in outcome in respect to the qualifications of the doctor (or nurse) in charge must also be considered.

One of the most important discoveries of the French inquiry pertains to the timing of accidents. During the induction of anaesthesia, 75 accidents and 9 deaths were recorded. For the maintenance period of anaesthesia, the figures are 81 accidents and 16 deaths, while 112 accidents and 42 deaths occurred during the postanaesthetic period.

The fact that more than half of all deaths occurred during the postoperative phase once more draws attention to the need for close supervision of the patients during recovery. It is in the light of this finding that another result of the study must be considered: only one third of all the patients went to a recovery room after surgery. The inquiry showed that recovery rooms with three beds on the average existed in 79% of the private nursing homes

78

(cliniques, privées). Recovery rooms were in use in 70% of all teaching hospitals (with 13 beds on the average), but only 56% of the non-teaching hospitals (4 beds on the average). The proportion of cases taken care of in the two kinds of institutions is 20% of all operations in teaching hospitals as against 30% in non-teaching institutions. As mentioned before, the private nursing homes take care of about half of all cases.

5. Anaesthesia administered by nurses

As in most countries on the continent, anaesthesia has been administered by students or nurses for a century in France. Anaesthesia has really evolved as a medical specialty only since the second world war. Before 1939 there were less than a dozen such specialists in Paris.

When the French anaesthesia society was founded in 1934, only four of its 100 members were practising anaesthetists. At present, the number of anaesthetists is approaching 8.000. Since they are involved not only in the practice of anaesthesia proper, but in intensive care, emergency medicine and pain treatment, they cannot take care of all cases in which anaesthesia is required. This is most obvious in small non-teaching hospitals with only two or three anaesthetists. For many years such hospitals were unable to attract any qualified physician anaesthetists or, at best, found only one. Even recently, an inquiry conducted by the anaesthesia-nurses' union demonstrated that up to 40% of all anaesthetics in non-teaching hospitals were given by nurses without immediate supervision. This state of affairs is now changing. Recently the administrative courts and, on appeal, the State Council have ruled that any accident occurring while a nurse is in change of the anaesthetic, with no physician-anaesthetist in attendance and physically present in the operating room, automatically involves the responsibility of the hospital. The concomitant financial burden is a strong incentive to seek more appropriate arrangements.

In the French inquiry, the rate of accidents did not differ when the anaesthetic was delivered by a doctor of by a nurse: 1,3 for 1000 anaesthetics for doctors; 1,4 per 1000 for nurses. The rate rose to 1,8 when doctors worked in relay, one starting the anaesthesic and another taking over later.

6. Informed consent

Any claim for damages must be backed up by evidence that such damage has occurred and that a causal link exists between the damage and the doctors' action. Moreover, it must be shown that the action was negligent or contrary to established rules of practice. The law does not implicate the doctors' responsibility in respect to the outcome but only in respect to the quality of care. It states that the doctor acting under normal circumstances is to care for the patient in a conscientious and attentive way and in conformity with established scientific rules. In addition, he is the one to give the patient appropriate information to enable him to choose among the various solutions or possible treatments. The information is to be given in a simple and loyal manner. In the event of a mishap, the patient who has not been forewarned of its possible occurrence may make a claim for damages as a result of insufficient information, stating that he would not have consented to the procedure if he was fully informed. In this way compensation may sometimes be obtained even if no fault by the doctors can be demonstrated in relation to the procedure involved.

Such claims have recently been made against anaesthetists on several occasions, involving mainly the choice between local and general anaesthesia.

7. The doctor-patient relationship

In addition to material interest, two errors appear to play a major role in influencing patients to sue doctors. The first is the doctors' tendency tobelittle risks in their initial conversation with patients and their reluctance to give a detailed account of possible mishaps. It should be noted in respect to the latter that the present-day tendency to praise medical accomplishments and emphasize scientific progress makes it difficult for patients or their relatives to accept at face value a statement from a doctor amounting to admission of ignorance. To admit that one does not know how to explain what has happened may appear to the doctor as a proof of honesty, it is usually interpreted by the patient as an attempt to hide some mistake. Only a full and honest presentation of the ever-possible complications during the pre-anaesthetic consultation offers a way out of this dangerous misunderstanding.

DISCUSSION

Crul: I would like to start the discussion with the topic of awareness, particularly the legal aspects of awareness. We will start with the lawyers. Although we anaesthetists have been faced with it over the last few years, this may be a new problem to them, and we will be interested to hear what they have to say. First of all, is every anaesthetist forced to promise a patient unconsciousness during every general anaesthetic? If you do, then of course it is a breach of promise when patients wake up, and that would be a very clear condition for legal action, would it not?

Wroblewski: In Germany we have not had any problems with awareness so far, but I am sure that just mentioning it will provoke some. I think in Germany the matter will be, whether the events leading to awareness were avoidable or unavoidable. You would have to prove that it was unavoidable in order not to be sued. There is a special German construction that you do not promise any success, you just promise your duty, your service. You are not sued because your were not successful, but because your service was not acceptable.

Crul: I think it is almost universal that you never promise a certain result as a doctor, but in the case of general anaesthesia, where consciousness is such a basic part, it might be looked upon as a breach of contract if a patient wakes up. In the opposite direction, we have had some cases in Holland where people have demanded to remain conscious during the operation because they felt it was a threat to them to sleep during the operation. Some people reacted so strongly to premedication particularly with benzodazepines, that they complained bitterly that they slept through the whole procedure or did not notice they had been operated on.

Wroblewski: As Dr. Hargrove mentioned, there are patients for whom you also have to use nitrous-oxide in order not to have them waken up.

A typical case might be in classical neurolept-anesthesia, where there is relaxation, analgesia, and hypnosis provided by dehydrobenzperidol. Sometimes the patients realize they are awake although they do not feel any pain; they hear noise but they do not feel any pain. The consequence could be that we will not be allowed to use classical neurolept analgesia, we will have to change to balanced anesthesia, always using a little bit of nitrous-oxide.

Marchetti: With neurolept analgesia the aim was to stay conscious, so it is thus different from balanced anaesthesia where sleeping is an essential part of the combination.

Crul: In the first years of neurolept analgesia, we intentionally kept the patients conscious. Later we added nitrous-oxide, and expected the patient to be asleep. Now we have gone back to pure analgesics, also for unconsciousness, but for some analgesics there is a threshold level over which, in some patients, you cannot make them more unconscious, even with the highest doses.

Palay-Vincent: I would like to ask about the importance of the damage caused by awareness.

Wroblewski: It depends on the psychological status of the patient. The typical relaxed type, as Dr. Hargrove said, will say "I heard everything, but it does not bother me at all". A very sensitive person will say "I did not feel any pain, but it hurt me for the next two or three years, I cannot get rid of it, and it will just be a nightmare for me". I think it is a very individual psychological reaction of every patient.

Palay-Vincent: That is true. The compensation is not very important, is it?

Wroblewski: Compensation can be a matter of importance, because you cannot prove that the patient was not damaged. It is completely subjective.

Hargrove: The damage, certainly in our cases, has been long-term psychological problems, which the patient had been able to prove. In the case I illustrated, Mrs. A. was able to convince the judge, that she could not face another pregnancy, so her family had been limited. The judge felt she deserved compensation for the fact that she could not complete her family, because of the psychological trauma. However, a little note in the paper two years later, said that Mrs. A. had had another baby by Caesarean section. This was after the award of the £ 13,000. She was actually able to find another anaesthetist in the same hospital to anesthetise her.

Palay-Vincent: The French courts want to see more concrete evidence. We have not had any cases like this yet.

Barrier: Probably one of the reasons why we do not have this kind of lawsuits in France is that there is extensive use of neurolept analgesia, probably more than in England and northern countries. However, we have problems with ventilatory depression in the recovery room, which, as Dr. Marchetti said, is a much greater danger than awareness. As a national witness I have 10 files in study, seven of them are of respiratory depression in the recovery room after neurolept analgesia with high doses and a wrong use of fentanyl analgesia.

Wroblewski: I think in Germany those kinds of problems will be very prone to lawsuits. Using neurolept anaesthesia or balanced anaesthesia with their well-known respiratory suppression problems, means that you have to make provisions for a safe recovery for the patient. If you do not do that, you are really likely to lose the case.

Lassner: May I take up the same problem in a different way? Let me remind Dr. Hargrove first of all of an old British definition of an anaesthetist, namely: "a gentleman half asleep bending over a gentleman half awake". Or the saying of the surgeon: "Sir, if your patient can stay awake, you should be able to do the same". This only demonstrates that it is probably not as new as we believe. I would like to remind you that in the early days of light ether anaesthesia, a level of anaesthesia where the patient was more or less awake, was the norm; the so-called "analgetic stage" of inhalation anaesthesia, which we have now more or less forgotten. Artusio rediscovered it 40 years later for cardiac surgery, and although it is 30 years old now, it is still the same principle.

I would like to address two points. One are the studies of recovery of memory after an anaesthetic, with psychological investigations using hypnosis. The most interesting observation comes from South Africa by a man named Levinson, who had done an experiment, exposing his patients to a sham accident. They all ran as follows: at a certain time during the operation the anaesthetist said in an anguished voice: "Stop surgery! Stop surgery! The patient is dying! This patient is all blue! I have to do something about it!". After a little while he says: "The patient seems to be better now. You can resume now, he is all right". Ten patients were exposed to this, during what seemed on the basis of the EEG monitoring a deep ether anaesthesia. Of these 10 patients later, 6 were able to recall and recover every single spoken word when brought under hypnosis. The 4 who did not, had a prolonged period of postoperative mental depression.

Then came a number of studies on postoperative depression, done by a group of men in Californa; David Cheek was one of them. He used another method of investigation under hypnosis to discover hidden incidents during anaesthesia, showing unexplained mental depression after operations. In a large number of cases very specific and clear-cut evidence was found that they had been able to hear and that - without having any normal recall - had been damaged psychologically by the fear they experienced during the operation.

Several years ago in my department we did similar investigations using hypnosis. There is no doubt, firstly, that - as has been known for more than a century - hearing is the last capacity of sensory activity which remains when brain function ceases, and the first to come back. I have been telling students for 40 years to "please speak to patients in a soft voice when they wake up, do not shout. The first sense which recovers is hearing, and nobody wants to be woken up by shouting". Secondly, there is a very interesting study by the late Milton Erikson from Phoenix, Arizona, which is extremely interesting to our understanding of sensory function. That - under hypnosis - you can have a selective blindness has been known for 200 years. There is also selective deafness. People under anaesthesia do not hear everything. They do hear things which are related and of importance to them. Therefore, the so-called trials of remembrance of music or things said to patients through earphones during anaesthesia and the fact that they are not found under hypnotic recall, does not have much meaning. The things played to them or told them were meaningless to them, while the terrible set of dramatic presentations by Levinson obviously would have impressed anybody when hearing it. Milton Erikson, attempted to find out how these things operate on himself and submitted himself to an ether anesthesia. He describes very vividly what he could recall and what not. It was always linked by importance to his safety or to his life. I therefore see and understand sensory experience in a new way. You must have heard it in the first place to discriminate, what is important and what not, but after having discriminated it, something disappears from memory, it is not stored. Pavlov's dog, in selectively not seeing the oval, but seeing the round form, is a different way of saying that not seeing is a selective mechanism. You have to see before not seeing, and you have to hear before not hearing. Therefore, all these experiences must take place at a time when the brain functions are sufficient for an EEG to show some kind of reaction.

Crul: Consciousness is of course one of the first things to disappear when brain function is interfered with. As we know from cardiac arrest, within 10 seconds unconsciousness develops, followed by the disappearance of all kinds of other reactions. If you have anaesthesized patients consciousness will come back earlier than all the other functions.

Lassner: Dr. Hargrove, I think you have described the treatment of the problem, telling us what you do with women coming for Caesarean section. You explain to them that consciousness, hearing, is an agreeable and interesting element of what is to happen. I have been doing the same in another experiment with relaxation. When Frances Foldes described his priming principle of dividing the doses of relaxants, obviously the risk exists that the patient notices and feels the early effects of relaxation, and could be frightened by them. I told my patients that their eyes may feel very heavy, they may not be able to swallow at all, they may feel difficulty in breathing. All this is as it should be and this is what they have to expect, because if it really occurs, this is a sign they are normal patients.

Hargrove: I think the whole point is to have adequate communication with the patient. You must have spoken with them beforehand. One of the things that came out of the recent workshop in Cardiff was to say that anaesthetists went even further than I did, in talking to the Caesarean section patients beforehand. Irrespective of whether it was an elective or emergency section, they spoke with the patients throughout the operation, assuming that they were partially awake, saying thinks like "You are doing very well, we are getting on nicely now, the baby is almost born". That is the next stage along. Are you going to do this for all patients having operations? Certainly the attitude of this meeting was, that we have got to re-educate ourselves and the surgeons to stop the sort of conversation that is going on in the operating room nowadays. Particularly the young doctors like to talk about their female conquests from the previous night, or the football scores, or this sort of things. It seems now that we have got to talk about optimistic things, regarding the outcome of the operation. We have loudspeakers in all the operating theatres, through which comes the result of the frozen biopsy sections. If for example you are in the middle of a breast biopsy, and a voice comes out of the wall which says "Yes, that is certainly malignant, I would cut it out". That must get through to the brain of the patient. There has been one case, where a woman heard the result of her own frozen section biopsy. We have got to re-educate ourselves as to what we say in the operating room.

Wroblewski: The example of awareness during the Caesarian section is a typical one of an avoidable mistake. Nevertheless, we do not avoid it, because we want to be on the safe side for the baby's sake. We always have to explain it to the patient in order not to get involved in a legal case.

Roos: Apart from the legal consequences, we did a small study in our hospital, in which we divided a group of patients into those to whom we gave every possible bit of information as to what could go wrong, and another group to whom we gave only very comforting information. The nurses did not know which patients were in which group, and they were asked to assess the patients' psychological condition after the pre-operative visits of the anaesthetists. We found that after the anaesthetists' visits patients in the fully informed group were quite anxious. What was surprising however, was that recovery from operation was accompanied by less complications and much quicker in the fully(-pestimistically) informed patients than in the comforted patients. Everything which was better than they had expected, gave them such a psychological lift that their recovery was much faster. We had them undergo psychological tests, to assess their state of anxiety and their sthenia. We found that the sthenic state of the patients who were given pessimistic information was much better; there was a three days' difference with the other group. If we tell the patient that he can expect some trouble, because we are not God and a hospital is not Heaven, and that he has to accept a certain amount of discomfort and at the same time assuring him that we do our very best to make the discomfort as small as possible, potential lawsuits are minimized, and we lessen the trouble of recovery for the patient.

Hallèn: It is certainly very comforting to hear, that we are acknowledging the psychological aspects of anaesthesia. From the complaints which I have studied, it seems to me that there is never just one reason for a complaint. In the majority of cases there is always a component of bad communication between the patient and the doctor. That is why I would like to ask all of the members of this panel what their attitude is towards the necessity of pre-anaesthetic communication between the anaesthetist and the patient. Are you enforced to do it, are you liable to critique afterwards if you have not done it, could you delegate the pre-anaesthetic consultation to someone else, or does the one responsible for the anaesthetic have to go to comfort, reassure, and study the case? In my country we behave badly in this matter, although we have to. Our boards seem to take this aspect more and more seriously. They demand that it should be done personally, but still this request is followed very poorly.

Lassner: I would like to answer this with two remarks. First of all, in France, the recommendation by the Ministry of Health specifies that the pre-operative examination by the anaesthetist is part of the anaesthetists' duty. As far as practice goes, this is always done in private clinics, except for emergencies. It may be a bit of a sham examination, but at least the anaesthetist comes in and speaks to the patient for a short while. In public hospitals it can be reduced to short visits too, but then, unfortunately, it is seldom done by the same individual who provides the anaesthetic the next day, because of their hours of duty in the hospital. In a number of hospitals now we have organized pre-anaesthetic clinics, where the patient is seen by an anaesthetist. Very often they are not the same as the one who will later give the anaesthesia and is only helped by the notes taken by the other. In public hospitals the patient risks to be treated like an object in a factory. One anaesthetist sees him when he comes in the pre-anaesthetic clinic, a second one may see him the night before and prescribe the premedication, a third may take care of him when he comes to the operating room, a fourth takes over during the operation, a fifth one sees him in the recovery room, and a sixth when he comes to autopsy. However, again, I would not say this is new. There is an old story of an anaesthetist comforting a patient who is a bit anxious before the operation, and says "Look, tomorrow when they put a needle into your vein, you will see me, and you will see my beard, then everything will fade. After a little while when you have slept, you will wake up and see me again, and you will recognize me by my beard". The patient finally wakes up and sees the bearded man and sees that this beard has grown and says "Has it lasted so long, doctor". The man then says "What do you mean by "doctor"? I am St. Peter!".

Crul: Mrs. Palay-Vincent, do you know of any cases found guilty because the anaesthetist did not see the patient before operation?

Palay-Vincent: Yes, that is often the problem. I am very interested in this aspect. Offering information to the patient seems to me fundamental and very important. When you speak with patients who plans to sue doctors, it is always the same story: they were not visited and nothing was explained to them. This is always the same refrain.

Lassner: Very often the initial reason for going to the police or to the prosecutor is to find out what really happened because the patients were not told what really happened.

Palay-Vincent: They say "Before the operation I saw everybody and after the accident I could not find the resident or the nurse or the doctor, so I went to the police station". It very often happens like that.

Crul: It is not reprisal they want, but it is information.

Barrier: I have a problem with a surgeon at the moment, a chief of department, because I always do a pre-anaesthetic consultation and I always do as Dr. Roos suggests, I answer all the patient's questions. The surgeon told me that he forbids me to tell all these awful things to his patients, because the patient will leave. I find it difficult to resolve this triangle of communication between surgeon, patient and anaesthetist with this particular surgeon.

Hargrove: The ideal is that the anaesthetist, who is going to anaesthetise the patient goes to see him beforehand. There are certain problems in British anaesthesia. For instance, I do not see all of my patients personnaly beforehand, but the anaesthetist who is with me on the operating list. I must admit that I am very privileged, we have two anaesthetists for every case; the other will always see the patient which I cannot see. The patients whom neither of us see, are those who come in as day cases. They are admitted to the hospital when I am already in the operating room, are seen by the duty anaesthetist, and they come up to the theatre; I have never seen them at all. They have been seen by an anaesthetist, but not by the one who will put them to sleep. The day cases are thus a major problem for us, because they are attached at the end of our operating lists.

Crul: I think day cases will also bring their own judicial problems, and they are increasing now with the financial costs of inpatient services. The problem is now how to provide pre-anaesthetic information to these patients and if possible by the same anaesthetist who will give the anaesthesia. Dr. Roos will cover this subject later in the workshop.

Hallèn: Just a short comment referring to Prof. Lassner referring to St. Peter. Some 10 years ago when my beard was still quite dark and I looked a bit more fierce perhaps, I anaesthetized a clergyman. When I spoke him a day or two later, he said to me "When I first woke up, I was extremely afraid, wondering where I had gone". This is an example of the distorted way of appreciating reality which our patients have. They really do not know where they are or what has happened.

Marchetti: Day cases are obviously arranged beforehand, so it should be possible to organize some pre-operative visits.

Hargrove: Our problem is that the surgeons put the patients down for day case admission. We do not know when that patient is coming until the day before, because that is when they are first scheduled on the operating list. It is a great problem for us; we would like to see them well beforehand. Changing the habits of surgeons may be a solution.

Manni: I think we all agree that one of the importang things is the personal approach of the anaesthetist to the patients, perhaps more important than pharmacological drugs. How is it possible to get this personal approach in a large hospital? If possible the same anaesthetist who will take care of the patient during the operation should visit the patient the day before and give him some explanation about the anaesthesia and the type of operation, but certainly it is a thing that needs time. Sometimes there is not sufficient time to do this well.

Crul: It has to do with the time at which the operating room schedules come out. In some hospitals, of course, they come out so late that the anaesthetist comes to the patient in the visiting hours for the family. Then it is very difficult to speak quietly with the patient, while all the relatives are there. One of the important things to enforce in a busy hospital is to have the programs ready by such a time that there is still ample time for the anaesthetist to do his rounds with the patients. We have a strict rule that all patients scheduled for Monday, who are already in the hospitals for investigation on Thursdays and Fridays are not allowed to go home before the anaesthetist has visited them, and only after that visit they may leave for the week-end. We consider the personal contact between patient and anaesthetist to be that important.

Roos: The system which in our opinion works quite nicely with day patients is that three or four afternoons a week a certain anaesthetist goes to the suites where the surgeons have their consultations, surgeons of all specialties. As soon as a surgeon states his intention to admit a patient as a day-care patient, he tells this to his assistant nurse, who then gives the patient some papers which include full anaesthetic instructions, information, and a do-it-yourself list of anamnesis.

The patient takes all of this home, and an appointment is made for him to go to the anaesthetist's pre-anaesthetic hour in the afternoon, where the anaesthetist then sees the patient and discuss with him/her what will be done. Also in the information is written, that due to the fact he is a day care patient, the anaesthetist who sees him at this visit will probably not anaesthetize him for the operation. He must state all his ailments or diseases clearly, state his preference for regional or general anaesthesia. He should understand that he must not drink alcohol for 24 hours after the operation, not use sewing machines or electric saws during that time, should leave contact lenses and diamonds at home, and that he has to have someone stay with him for 24 hours after getting home. He must tell the anaesthetist if he lives more than one flight of stairs up without an elevator. Then he has to sign a piece of paper which is at the bottom of the written information, stating that he has read and understood all the information, will stick to the rules, and wishes to be a day care patient. That works quite well. In my lecture later in the workshop I'll describe it more extensively.

Lassner: May I suggest that you provide us with a copy of this so that we may add it to our report? (Note: See further on.)

Crul: Perhaps we should now draw our attention to discussing the extensive use of opioids during anaesthesia. What would you require in the way of surveillance after anaesthesia in cases in which there is a danger of post-operative respiratory depression or complete apnoea? Should you require anything special and for how long after anaesthesia? Dr. Marchetti told us that with the newer drugs the time in which you may fear resporatory arrest is much shorter than with the older ones. One might say "Well, supervision only for one or two hours, that is enough", but some of the respiratory depressions, particularly now with epidural or spinal administration of opioids, occur up to five, six, seven, or eight hours afterwards.

Marchetti: I do not agree with you, Prof. Crul.The epidural administration of fentanyl has given some very early respiratory depressions. Yet I think it is a very safe manner of administration of this drug. No delayed effects have been observed with epidural fentanyl after the first hour or two. Morphine is different, some respiratory depression was described about four days after epidural administration. I think it is due to the pharmacokinetic properties of morphine, particularly the low lipophylicity.

Crul: I do not want to go into a discussion of the different pharmacological properties of opioids. It is the general legal problem of what to demand in the way of supervision of anaesthetic cases which have had pain relief by analgesics, morphine or any of the newer ones. Just the legal consequences.

Wroblewski: This is a big topic to discuss, because so far we have not had any cases brought to court. I might give you some ideas as to what the court would think if there were. I think with such a life-threatening complication the court will decide that you must do everything possible to protect the patient. Even a very long-term or very small potential danger of a life-threatening complication would put you in difficult position. On the other hand, you might be forced to use other means of analgesia if you are not able to provide a safe system for surveillance of the patient. Just those two points might indicate that there is a lot to be discussed in the case. It also makes a difference, whether you are doing it for a operation or for the painrelief in terminal cancer patients. It can be a matter of discussion, whether at the end of life you should enable the patient to live the remainder of his life at home comfortably. If such a life-threatening danger of respiratory depression exists, but you are taking that risk, it would not look rosy for you in court, particularly if you had used that technique for a younger patient, who had minor post-operative pain. The court should say: was it not preferable to provide analgesia with other drugs, free from this side effect? There are a lot of things in each individual case, which must be considered.

Crul: There must be a calculated risk, before some one can be excused.

Lassner: There have been a number of cases of respiratory arrest after the general use of opioids. I am not speaking now about epidural or spinal administration. A number of anaesthetists have been convicted in France, one with a six months' suspended prison term, for having given a large dose of phenoperidine for a cystoscopy and laparoscopy. The patient spoke to the anaesthetist and to the surgeon after the operation and was sent back to her room. Her husband sat with her, she was very quiet, and finally the nurse came in to find the patient dead. These cases have come to trial, and, as Dr. Wroblewski pointed out, the anaesthetist is in very grave danger himself, if he is unable to explain why he let the patient go back to her room, where obviously no competent and continuous supervision was present even after having apparently regained consciousness. The anaesthetist would have had to know, that, what he had been doing would risk the patients' existence. I had the same problem in my department many years ago when we started using epidural opioids. We could not organize recovery room type of surveillance for the whole afternoon and night for every patient, who would otherwise not have gone to the recovery room. We restricted the use because it was not possible to ensure that they would get appropriate care post analgesia.

Crul: I may illustrate the occurrence of post analgesia respiratory depression by a little survey, I did myself some 30 years ago in a private hospital in the south of Holland, where I had then been working at that time. For about a month I went through all the night reports of the surgical wards and I picked out all cases in which the nurse had stated "Patient found dead in bed". I looked back at the time at which a narcotic analgesic had been given for pain relief, and almost all of them had received a narcotic withing an hour before they were found dead. Because of lack of supervision after administration of opioids the cases of respiratory depression must have been much more frequent at that time than either of us suspected.

Barrier: I would like to speak about a kind of case which is becoming more and more frequent in France. It is the case of functional surgery, tympanoplasty for example. This kind of surgery is done with microsurgical procedures and it takes a long time. Yet it is nog felt to be life-threatening, neither by the patient and family nor by the nurses. The patient receives a large amount of narcotics, and only receives short recovery surveillance. As an expert witness I now have six files of tympanoplasty patients with respiratory arrest two hours after surgery, however the nurses considered them to be minor surgery patients and sent them back to the ward shortly after surgery. They received a large amount of narcotics for surgery, which lasted for three or four hours. After three hours the patient begins to bleed a little in the ear, the surgeon asks for more anaesthesia, so they have a second shot of opioid just before the end of the operation. In each of the cases it happened after this was done, that there was a respiratory accident. I had no such cases before last year.

Hargrove: I would like to make just two small points. One is to briefly dismiss this question of epidural opiates. We have made it a rule that every patient having epidural opiates goes to the intensive care unit. We cannot have them going back to the wards. They go there for 24 hours. The second point is that the biggest problem we have with high dose opiates peri-operatively is that frequently at the end of the operation the junior anaesthetist is not willing to wait, and gives naloxone to reverse the respiratory depression. The patient is then returned to the recovery room breathing well, but in severe pain. The nurses in the recovery then give him another dose of an opiate and send him back to the ward in a comfortable state. That is when you get the syndrome of "death in bed". This is the big problem. They reverse the opioid with a short-acting drug like naloxone and after a short while the respiratory depression returns.

PROBLEMS OF SURGICAL AND ANAESTHETIC ABSTINENCE: LEGAL AND ETHICAL CONSEQUENCES

L. René

To abstain from interfering surgically or anaesthesically is an important decision from an ethical and legal point of view. But in certain cases it is legitimate. The problem is the same when, after a succession of complications, we hesitate over the decision to interrupt the escalade of interventions (which, - let's state it clearly - does not mean: not to give medical attention). In both cases this decision cannot be taken in isolation but by the whole team, consisting of members which act together.

This team is at the service of the patient, to give him medical attention, cure him if possible, bring him relief, respecting his dignity as a human being. To know when to interfere or abstain implies an unfailing technical background, but also a long practise and a solid culture, both medical and human: a choice unsufficiently enlightened and thought over would fail in the ethical justification.

In most cases abstaining is a decision which imposes itself on the members of the team: the present medical knowledge and the specific circumstances of the case under consideration dictate the medical decision, which must be conscentious and attentive, prudent and diligent.

But there are cases when the members of the team have a different opinion of the situation, which leads to a discussion between them. This ends in either a joint decision, or a split decision and, to keep to our subject, we will start by studying three situations and see, from a moral and legal point of view, what the effects of a joint decision to abstain are. Then we will study the abstention, but now as a result of an unresolvable disagreement. It is an exceptional eventuality with heavy consequences.

Here are the three cases - exemplary but quite different in their moral and legal consequences - of a joint decision to abstain.

I. The decision to abstain surgically must take into account the will of the patient, who must be conscious and clearly, and truthfully informed of the situation, of the risks and benefits of the intervention planned. This is always possible with a clear-minded patient, except in particularly urgent situations. In fact, experience shows that most often the patient "relies" on us. But the ethical rule is categorical: surgeons and anaesthesists must, as all doctors, respect the refusal of a patient who is conscious and informed of the situation. The current rules of deontology in the western world and the recommendations of the European organizations as well as jurisprudence, all agree on this point.

One problem is: the patient is unable to state his will clearly either because of cerebral lesions or because of troubled judgement. Psychiatrists do know those difficult situations during the acute phase of the illness. Surgeons and anaesthetists face them too. Common sense, the agreement of the family, and a favourable prognosis help to interprete the letter of the law: I have never heard of a patient cured in spite of himself taking legal action.

In the same logic, to obtain a consensus of abstention by way of essentially dishonest information must be condemned by the moralist and the judge. Such an aberration, as exceptional as it seems, has still taken place.

II. Can a surgeon and an anaesthetist give up pursuing the usual treatment when the patient has put himself in their hands for this pursuit of the cure by saying "I rely on the doctor"?. Isn't this the dilemma arising when all the efforts undertaken to cure or to relieve have failed? A huge divergence of opinion has followed the great progress in techniques, their successes and side-effects (which we cannot deny), their psychological impacts and the recent questioning of the previously secure philosophical conception of human life.

Moreover, the use of inadequate terms is misleading: this is quite obvious concerning our subject.

a. In the name of what principle can we criticize the surgeon or the anaesthetist who refuses to pursue a treatment that the illness has rendered hopeless? A surgeon is never obliged to prolong the agony by technical prowess. When the game is lost, any therapeutical act being painful for the patient would be inhuman. I think it is wrong to use the word "euthanasia" to refer to that abstention. Especially because a doctor can still bring an important help at the very moment when he refuses to obstinately pursue the actual treatment. Let's take a closer look.

b. Morally as well as legally, the surgeon can rightfully abstain from operating while the anaesthesist keeps struggling against the physical pain, the discomfort and the distress of such patients.

This means avoiding the risks of therapeutical accidents, all the more severe as they occur on a weak ground. Some are even fatal. The most rigid moralists - f.i. Pope Pius XII as early as 1949 - accept such attitudes, even if they may cut short a life already hopelessly endangered. That therapeutically palliative attitude entails risks but cannot be seen as being "euthanasia".

The debate is not a difficult one as long as it remains theoretical. The infinite variety of specific cases makes it impossible to be dogmatic.

c. There is now a third meaning given to the word "euthanasia": deliberately provoking death (pity killing). This supposes a deliberate action on the part of the doctor and not a mere abstention. This is called active euthanasia. However, this leads us away from our subject. Let's just say that, in France, this is a crime but subject to attenuating circumstances.

It is easy to understand how much the problem of surgical and anaesthesiological abstention is obscured by the use of ambiguous terms.

III. But we must now consider a third possibility: the situation is entirely different when the patient is in peril - a most extreme form of danger- and can be helped by a doctor's action. For such a person in peril abstaining would be an extreme fault. That moral rule, illustrated two thousand years ago by the biblical parabol of the Good Samaritan, became in France, forty years ago,. a legal obligation. Refusal to come to the help of a person in need is a punishable offence. That humanitarian rule applies to each citizin, so to doctors too. But not to them only, as it was once feared.

Moreover we must not misunderstand the meaning of "refusal to come to the help": it does not demand an unreasonable therapeutical insistence. French jurisprudence is clear: frightened by a few misinterpreted legal decisions, some doctors have thought they would be guilty in the eye of the law if they do not do everything possible to save a life in spite of the poor patient's condition, the stage of illness, the human side-effects of the pathological episodes and the patient's lucid and informed attitude towards the envisaged intervention and reanimation. There is no ethical justification for inhuman and probably hopeless therapeutic tenacity.

Up to now we have envisaged only situations where the team has reached a consensus before acting on a joint decision. But there are unfortunately cases where no agreement is reached.

We should emphasize how a discord within the team - openly demonstrated to the paramedical staff - is a dangerous attitude: the prestige of the team and the confidence that the patient has in it are the first victims. In the case of legal proceedings the climate thus created would be very unfavourable: the court doctors will be unfavourably impressed and no doubts will be severe with all the doctors of the team torn by discord, if not passions: the judges would rightly consider that the quality of the care could only have suffered. So much for the legal consequences.

But what of the ethical situation?

As always, things are more complicated if we must evaluate intentions. One example to illustrate:

According to current deontology we must abstain each time the treatment calls for greater competence or means (including the material conditions) than can be supplied by the practician. This is to guarantee the quality of the treatment. It is appropriate, then, to appeal to outside competence. But in the heat of action we make a very subjective estimation of the moment at which we exceed our possibilities. Difficulties may arise from divergent estimation of the competences and abilities of the various active members of the team. Personality and emotions can interfere and bring on explosive situations: with Professor Lassner we have seen such situations in the course of an exploratory mission, but we were unable to propose a solution, which was fair and yet conformed to the laws and rules, because of the current rigidity of the status of medical personnel in public hospitals.

In practice two opposed situations can arise. During an urgent intervention already under way we cannot morally envisage a brutal interruption of a necessary cooperation. On the other hand, if it is a question of non urgent therapeutic progression, which is still at the project stage, a reasoned decision and a declaration to abstain on the part of one of the participants is acceptable: such an attitude can be justified by invoking a "clause of conscience". But the repetition of such decisions would quickly compromise the existence of the team and would undermine the efficiency of the team leader, whether he be surgeon or anaesthesist. Yet, let's add that fifteen days ago a decision of the Cour de Cassation "toutes chambres réunies" (the highest French judiciary authority) stated precisely the jurisprudence. It entrusts the surgeon with the responsability of coordinating and watching over the whole medical team.

Happily, total disagreement is exceptional. In practice, anaesthesist and surgeon act together for the benefit of the cure: its efficacity depends on their good understanding and their complementary behaviour.

DISCUSSION

Lassner: Prof. René pointed out the importance of the image of the physician in the eyes of the public. They appear very united and avoid the grave consequences of an open conflict. Most often it is the surgeon suggesting active surgical treatment, while the anaesthetist is the one who steps on the breaks or tries to prevent him from operating. The other possibility: the anaesthetist suggesting an operation and the surgeon not wanting to do it, does also occur and has come up many times. I think we should consider these two things separately. To specify my own thoughts on it, I would like to tell a small story of a surgeon, who, after having been Surgeon General in the navy, turned to private practice. We knew each other from our naval days. One day he asked me to anaesthetize one of his patients, and added "This is an order to kill". We had a short chat on orders in the relationship between physicians, whether inside or outside the navy, and a second chat on what it would mean to accept such an order. The main point was that, if one accepts an order to kill, one should be a professional in it. This has existed in human society for a long time, but it is not medically acceptable. On the other hand, if one has good reasons to believe that the other partner in the medical team has blinded himself to that kind of situation, then we should really take the situation out of its acute stressful dramatic aspect and sit down and discuss it. However, this dispute takes place usually on the spot, with nobody even thinking about it. I believe we have all been in the situation where an anaesthetist had accumulated evidence to show that a surgeon had blinded himself for many months or years to the complications of his own surgery and steadfastly refused to have reoperations done by himself or others, when complications arose. This exists, but on the other hand it has become a kind of attitude for some younger colleagues in anaesthesia to be able to stand up against the wishes of the surgeon and deny him anaesthesia. They feel so pleased with themselves, since for once they are the ones who can say "No". This is a very poor attitude. In France it has very deep roots, and I would like to say one word about it. In Europe, surgeons as you can remember, were out of the scientific profession of medicine for several centuries as it was forbidden by the church to cure with iron or fire. When they were finally admitted back in, a bit through the back door I must say, they were first right to assert themselves. In the nineteenth century, when surgery developed in a new way particularly after the introduction of anaesthesia and the discovery of antisepsis, they became the very image of active and successful medicine at a time when internal medicine was still rather poor in its cures. As is usual with

97

98

the newly rich, they behaved like the newly rich. They were overbearing and rather unpleasant in temper. Had they not been dramatic in attitude, they would probably not have become surgeons in the first place. For several decades these overbearing surgeons would not tolerate an active and equal partner, they had to work with underlings, as that was what they were used to. When this situation changed the underlings tried to outdo the surgeons. In France, the anaesthetists invented a trick. They told everybody else but the surgeons, that the surgeons were not curing but agressing the patient. It was taught that the only one who would protect the patient was the anaesthetist, thanks to his special knowledge and methods of protection. I have said many times that protectionism was not any better in medicine than in economics. It always ended up in failure. To claim and teach protectionism is regression, stupidity. It is self-satisfaction on pseudomoral grounds. It has to be eliminated. We have to look the thing straight in the face. We are not the "good" ones and the surgeons the "bad" ones. We are partners. We have to give polite, good care, but we cannot outdo, what can be done. If we admit this -I feel- we have to forget the fight against the surgeons, but the surgeons should somehow help us to forget it, because it is not always simple.

René: In the last years of the nineteenth century, the faculty taught surgeons that it was very difficult to become a good surgeon, but very easy to remain it, and this is the thought of a great number of surgeons. Deontologically and ethically the anaesthetist has the right and the duty to refuse to work with an incompetent surgeon. Even in the last two weeks I had to reply to an anaesthetist, that he had no obligation to anaesthetize for an imcompetent surgeon.

Palay-Vincent: When anaesthetists and surgeons have exclusive contracts with clinics, and the anaesthetists refuse to work with a surgeon because they consider him incompetent, it is difficult to break the contract. Now, whenever I make a contract between the two, I always say that exclusivity is not practical.

Crul: This exclusivity was born out of history, of course that is from the time that there were not enough specialists. The more there were the less need there was to have such exclusivity. Nowadays, of course, it can be the other way around, and also that should not happen.

May I just say one more thing about abstinence? A few years ago I attended a surgical meeting in which all of the surgical specialties were combined and we discussed the ultimate borders of operability of patients. What could you do and what could you not do? For that meeting I studied the ultimate borders of acceptance for anaesthesia. I looked back over five years of anaesthesia in my own department, some 67,000 anaesthetics, and studied those deaths in which retrospectively I felt it would have been a better decision to refuse anaesthesia. I came to only three or four death in patients with respiratory problems and three cases of death by circulatory problems in which, I felt, it would have been justified to refuse anaesthesia. In all those tens of thousands of cases, there are indeed a very limited number in which we anaesthetists would have done better to deny any help. On the other hand - and I could not answer this question at that time - which should be our criteria to refuse categorically anaesthesia to a patient? Is it the 50-50 chance of killing the patient right at induction? Should it be less? Should it be more? This is that kind of critical area, in which for us anaesthetists it is always very difficult to be absolutely certain of our justification to refuse cooperation. I have seen many anaesthetists, particularly those working in smaller hospitals, who solve it by taking on an authorative attitude and say "no" if they think it is going to be difficult. They do not argue with the surgeons, they just put in the full weight of their independent specialty and simply say how they think and that is it. I think we should try to avoid that, but do as Professor Lassner and Professor René said, and sit down, consider the urgency and necessity of the operation and all the chances of dangerous assaults done to the patient by either the surgeon or the anaesthetist and then try to come to a joint conclusion.

Manni: I would like to know from the colleagues of the different countries, what happens when sometimes there are problems between the surgeons and the anaesthetists about establishing whether an operation is a real emergency. Sometimes in my hospital, there is some competition between surgeons and anaesthetists about this. If this situation occurs in your hospital, what do you do? In Italy the surgeon always has the last word.

Roos: I would like to extend on that question. Is it not so that the patient or the relatives of the patient have the last word, and the surgeons or the anaesthetist can only give very strong advice in one direction or another? However, if a surgeon and an anaesthetist together come to the conclusion that abstaining would be beneficial, and the patient or a relative still insists on the operation, whould the surgeon or the anaesthetist not comply with those wishes? On the other hand, if the surgeon and the anaesthetist say that there is a great risk, but they feel they should do it, is the patient not the one who has the ultimate word?

Palay-Vincent: Undoubtedly, you must refuse intervention if you think it is bad for the patient. The will of the patient can be retained in that hypothesis.

My feeling is that if you think it is better for a patient not to be operated, you have to refuse.

Wroblewski: If the patient says "I do not want to be operated on", that is the last word. On the other hand, if he wants to be operated on, it is not automatically that you have to operate. It is your medical opinion to do so or to leave it. In Germany we have a special agreement between the professional body of surgeons and anaesthetists, which gives the last word to the surgeons. I personally do not think it is the best solution. If the surgeon says that there is an indication for operating, we are obliged to cooperate, except when we could prove that there is abuse of the right of the last word. This, I think, will never happen. I think the problem in our view is that there is always statistical evidence supporting every case. What makes arguing so difficult is, that every surgeon knows of a very old person with the same or similar problems, which he successfully solved surgically. This is difficult psychologically, as there are two levels you are comparing, individual fate and statistical truth.

Hallèn: I would like to comment on this question in two ways. Of course, for good cooperation we should sit down together as sensible, intelligent people, and we will almost almost solve it. It is rare nowadays that we do not. Of course collision can occur. The best thing to do, at least in a system like ours, is to refer to the next man in command, and thus the very tricky problems should always be dealt with by a very senior surgeon and very senior anaesthetist. If it still happens, and I have only encountered it a very few times, I have a little trick of my own. Of course, I am not an expert in surgery, so I rarely can contest with him completely. What I do is, I almost ceremoniously take out my fountain pen and write into the journal or the diary or the progress notes of the patient that Mr. (Surgeon) so-and-so directly requests of me an anaesthetic in spite of my sincere advice against doing so. I then ask the surgeon to sign it, and say that only then will I do it. It must be stated, that it is in spite of very direct warnings, that the surgeon requested the anaesthetist to do it. In all three cases in which I have used this, the surgeon backed down, when he had to declare it in this way. In my country no one can in any way force a doctor to do anything against his conscience and knowledge, not even a patient and not even a surgeon.

Hargrove: I would agree with Dr. Hallèn on this. You have to sit down and discuss the matters together. In the United Kingdom it is rather nice, because the final decision always rests with the anaesthetist. If we say "no", then "no" it is. However, we have to be very sure of the grounds upon which we say "no". The first ground is lack of competence to deal with the problem at hand by the anaesthetist, in other words, a very junior anaesthetist can say, that he will not tackle a certain problem. He should do as Dr. Hallèn says, that is to move the problem up the scale so that someone else can take it on. The next ground is that we can honestly say a patient is not in the best possible physical condition for the operation. Obviously, in the case of a woman with an ectopic pregnancy who is bleeding profusely, then you will get on and do the operation in spite of the patient being desperately ill. However, if you have, say, a small baby with pyloric stenosis, and the surgeon considers it to be an emergency, but the baby does not have normal electrolytes, you are perfectly in your right to refuse on the grounds, that the baby is not in the best possible physical condition. Our other problem arises where there is a conflict between the law and ethics, and this occurs in terminations of pregnancy. We have an abortion law, and certain criteria must be fulfilled before an abortion may take place. An anaesthetist and a gynecologist often look at that law from a different viewpoint, and, again, the anaesthetist has the option to withdraw. It is the same in France and in Holland, I guess.

Wroblewski: In Germany a doctor can be punished if his medical treatment of a patient is absolutely wrong, even when demanded by the patient. An extreme example, which of course never happens, would be that a patient says he wants his hand cut off because he has headaches. If the doctor does it he will be punished. We thus have a penalty law which says it is immoral.

Lassner: The same exists in France for sexual disfigurements. You are not permitted to take a man's genitals off, because he asks you to do so.

Roos: The necessity of agreement between anaesthetist and surgeon was stressed, and I fully agree with that. However, I have often come to cases where the surgical procedure was not really too difficult, but the anaesthetic difficulties were far greater and the surgeon had not spoken with the patient about the risks involved with the anaesthesia. In principle you should always come to the patient as a united front. I still think, and I would like to hear your opinion on it, that the duty to the patient comes first; as an anaesthetist you do have to inform the patient of the risk of anaesthesia, even if the surgeon does not agree. As an example I mention a Hartmann's procedure, which is done in three stages. Two stages were finished, so the patient was automatically placed on the operating list six months later for the third stage of the operation, but in the meantime he had two severe myocardial infarcts and a cerebrovascular accident. The anaesthetist thought it was his duty to inform the patient and the patient's relatives about the added risks of this new anaesthesia, and then they had a consultation with the cardiologist. By him the patient was told he had only one more year to live. He said that he could live perfectly well with his stoma, so he did not want to have the operation. The surgeon brought the case before the ethical committee. How do you feel about that kind of case?

Wroblewski: I do agree with your approach to the problem, that the patient's word must be final. We should certainly avoid the danger of fighting in front of the patient, or of putting the responsibility of both anaesthesia and surgery upon the shoulders of the patient. Sometimes we leave the patient aside, and I think that should never happen. I think if the patient demands all the information about the risk, we must give it to him, but if we realize that he is anxious and really worried, maybe the decision should be made between the surgeon and the anaesthetist. The procedure in our clinic is that we, anaesthetists, never talk about the surgical problems, and the surgeon never talks about the anaesthetic problems.

Crul: This is correct and maintains impartiality, that way we do not induce something which your partner does not really mean.

Hallén: There is always a trick when you have a difficult problem, and that is to expand it. I would like to ask the feelings of our colleagues about one problem that occasionally arises in the cooperation between surgeons and anaesthetists, the problem of the choice of anaesthetic technique. Does it not often happen that the surgeon sees the patient in his or her interview with the patient and "promises" a certain type of anaesthetic? Then one or two days later the anaesthetist comes and finds a general anaesthetic completely unsuitable, and then you have a problem.

In the material I presented, there is quite a number of cases where the real reason for the complaint was just this: the patient thought he was going to have one type of anaesthesia and then was persuaded by the anaesthetist to have another type. What about the right to choose the anaesthetic method? To whom does that belong? What is actually the situation in the different countries?

Hargrove: The decision in the United Kingdom is entirely that of the anaesthetist. I think it is a question of educating the surgeons to think along these lines. They have the absolute right to decide what surgical procedures they are going to use, and the anaesthetists have the absolute right to decide what anaesthetic procedures they are going to use. It is a question of education and only very occasionally you see on our operating lists, for instance, the name of the patient, the operation, and in brackets "spinal" or "epidural" put after it. If that happens without the consent of the anaesthetist, there is usually a very big argument. We would not tolerate the suggestion from the surgical side of how to do the anaesthesia.

Crul: That is my idea, too. The only thing that we should be sure of is to provide optimal conditions for the surgery involved, but how you reach this, you must decide for yourself. Nobody should interfere with that, because if things go wrong you are fully to blame for what you have done, and you cannot hide behind a suggestion from the surgeons. No court will take that as an excuse, not in my country and not in yours either, I suppose.

Lassner: The way Dr. Hargrove described the situation is common in France too, yet I am not too happy with it. When an anaesthetist has worked with a particular surgeon for many years, he knows his preferences and his abilities and then I feel that the anaesthetist is perfectly free to comment on the method of surgery. The same also goes for the surgeon, if he knows the anaesthetist well. He could say that - if he could choose between spinal and general anaesthesia - he feels for this or that reason that he would prefer to operate under spinal anaesthesia. I cannot see any good reason why they should not consider themselves as partners able to discuss these things. We separate our territories the way dogs do, and this is not the best way to approach human and neither professional relationships.

Crul: What I mean by providing the ideal conditions for the surgeon to do the operation is, that if he can convince you that with a certain type of anaesthesia he can do a better job, then you have to consider it very seriously, of course. But he cannot say that just because he has promised that to the patient. It should be a choice based on what is the best care for the patient.

Lassner: There is a third problem, which you probably remember, Dr. Hargrove. Surgeons used to send the patients to see an internist or cardiologist and were provided with a recommendation by the cardiologist to give plenty of oxygen, or just a note to say that he is fit for anaesthesia. I published a paper on this, which in French says "Those who councel are not those who have to pay for it". I said to the cardiologist "If you want to do this operation under oxygen, please do so, you do not need me".

Wroblewski: These examples should remind us that anaesthetists are responsible for what they do. It would never be a problem to discuss this with the surgeon if you work in a friendly atmosphere. It still must be up to the anaesthetist to decide solely what to do, because he is responsible. I think it is more a political question to leave it so strongly structured like it is at present.

Hargrove: I would agree with Prof. Lassner from the point of view of those cases, which are being done by a surgical team that have worked together for years. However, the vast majority of anaesthetics in the United Kingdom will be given by registrars or junior staff, who do not belong in a team because they might be working with one surgeon one week and a different one the next. One of our big problems is that the obstetricians will say to a patient that of course she can have her Caesar under epidural, when she may be totally the wrong sort of person to have that type of anaesthesia. We then have to explain to the patient that she cannot have it under epidural, because it is not the right thing for her. This then makes the obstetrician look stupid in the eyes of the patient. Therefore, it is so important that they do not say anything to the patient about the methods of anaesthesia until we have had a chance to see them. It is a constant problem at home. It occurs because there are not constant teams for every single operation.

Lassner: I have legal experience with such a case in France. A surgeon told a patient that he would have a very light anaesthetic, just a touch of it. He meant in fact local anaesthesia on this occasion; brachial plexus block. This was given, but nerve damage supervened and the case came to court. Initially the recommendation was the surgeon's, but the anaesthetist was quite obviously involved in the outcome.

Wroblewski: I think it is a very good example for the fact that if something with the anaesthesia goes wrong, you are fully responsible. It should be completely up to the anaesthetist to decide. In our clinic we have no problem with this, the surgeons never say a word about anaesthesia, it is completely up to us and it will stay so.

Lassner: I have been promulgating regional anaesthesia in France for about 30 years, but there have been many cases, where the surgeon has objected on different grounds, for example, because he could not talk about bridge games. I feel we should not live on the basis of a permanent divorce. We have to sleep together.

LEGAL AND ETHICAL PROBLEMS OF ANAESTHESIA FOR ORGAN TRANSPLANTATION

C. Manni

Organ transplantation is certainly one of the most complex problems the anaesthesiologist has had to face over the last few years. The problem is complex, not only from the medical point of view, but also from the deontological, ethical and legal points of view.

In practice, the anaesthesiologist finds himself acting as the arbitrator in a plainly conflicting situation; on one hand there are the often pressing needs of patients, whose survival and quality of life depends on the possibility of undergoing organ transplants; on the other hand, there is need to respect the rights of patients suffering from suspected brain death and of patients' relatives. These opposing requirements have not yet permitted the establishment of universally-accepted guidelines for the surgeon and the anaesthesiologist to follow during the complex sequence of events leading up to the transplantation of an organ.

The first point of controversy concerns the defining of a possible organ donor. The reply to this question would appear simple: any patient who is in a state of brain death can be considered a possible organ donor. However, in practice the problem is extremely complicated and calls for a more thorough analysis of the ethical and legal problems involved.

We all know that by "brain death" we mean the autolysis of the hemispheres and of the brain stem, i.e. the complete and irreversible destruction of the whole intracranial contents. A patient in a state of brain death is undoubtely dead, both from the biological and legal point of view, even if some of his organs (heart, kidney, lever) still maintain normal functions. Thus, there is no doubt that a patient in a state of brain death is a potential organ donor. However, we doctors have rightly asked ourselves another question: is it really necessary for the whole brain to be affected by the process of autolysis in order to make a diagnosis of clinical death? Or, is it not sufficient for the acception of clinical death that there is a definite irreversible lesion, which includes the key areas responsible for a normal functioning of the central nervous system?

At present, this reasoning is formulated for two well-known pathological conditions:

1. a persistent vegetative state or "appalic syndrome"
2. a coma arising from an irreversible lesion of the brain stem.

A persistent vegetative state is characterized by the inability to react appropriately to any external stimuli, even though an adequate cardio-respiratory function is maintained. There are numerous etiological mechanisms: bilateral destruction of the cerebral cortex (as often observed following prolonged cardiac arrest), bilateral hemispherical demyelinasation (which sometimes follows carbon monoxide poisoning or a traumatic lesion), extensive bilateral lesions of the corpus striatum or paramedian lesions of the reticular formation of the mesencephalon or of the posterior diencephalon.

A coma from an irreversible lesion of the brain stem is, in most cases, the result of ischemic-hemorrhagic lesions. The complete destruction of the brain stem structures is accompanied by absence of spontaneous respiration and is not compatible with a long-term survival despite resuscitative measures.

As far as a persistent vegetative state is concerned, a diagnosis of clinical death would be justified, owing to the loss of the psycho-physical unity of the individual. In other words, the quality of life appears so compromised as to loose all explicit or determinable meaning. However, it is not yet possible to establish with certainty the irreversibility of this type of lesion. Progressive albeit slow improvement in the condition of the brain have been reported by many neurologists and other doctors in intensive care units. In cases as these, our objective should be to learn which instrumental and pharmacologic treatments are capable of promoting the recovery of neurons, which are compromised functionally but are anatomically intact. Discontinuing the life-support system for such patients, would be an act of euthanasia that cannot be justified - not even by plans for a transplant -.

The reasons which permit us to declare a patient dead with a complete and irreversible lesion of the entire brain stem (even if a partial activity of the cortical neurons persists) are very different. Not only has clinical experience, in fact, shown us that this type of lesion is incompatible with survival. Despite instrumental and pharmacological treatments, these patients die within a few hours or, at the very most, within a few days. It could not be otherwise when one bears in mind the fact that the centres regulating all the vital functions of the organism (cardiac, respiratory and metabolic) are located in the brain stem.

In view of this, it is likely that in the near future a hypothesis will be considered valid, which says that a complete and irreversible structural lesion of the entire brain stem (brain stem death) is the equivalent of death of the entire organism, even when there is a residual partial activity of some cortical neurons. At present, however, this hypothesis requires further verification and as far as our country is concerned, we prefer to define death only when there is a complete and irreversible destruction of the entire contents of the cranial cavity (brain death).

Another point of controversy arises from the criteria for ascertaining brain death. There is unanimous agreement that the necessary conditions for an irreversible arrest of the cerebral functions are as follows:

1. state of coma
2. absence of reflexes from the brain stem (light, corneal and oculovestibular reflexes)
3. absence of motor response in the areas innervated by the cranial nerves
4. absence of spontaneous respiration in the presence of $PaCo_2$ equal to or exceeding 40 mmHg
5. absence of electrical cerebral activity.

There is disagreement on how long the above mentioned clinical and instrumental criteria should persist: the period must be sufficiently long to allow, beyond a shadow of doubt, a certain diagnosis of brain death.

The wish to reduce the observation time is dictated by the need to prevent the deterioration of organs which could be transplanted. At present in Italy, the law dictates an observation period of 12 hours. In actual fact, this period tends to be reduced because experience has shown that the symptoms of areflexia and apneic coma, with absence of electrical cerebral activity, do not regress unless the coma has been caused by endocrino-metabolic imbalances or by pharmacologic intoxication.

In the case of primary and structural lesions of the Central Nervous System an observation period of 6 hours thus appears more than sufficient and this reduced period has been proposed in a new law dealing with the removal of body parts for transplant purposes. This proposal has already been approved by one of the two chambers of the Italian Parliament.

At present, an observation period of less than 6 hours would not appear sufficient to exclude categorically the possibility of error. New proposals can be put forward in the future when we will have more sophisticated and efficient diagnostical techniques at our disposal.

Another cause of debate and heated controversy is the approach made to the legal representatives of potential donors (family members or others) to seek their <u>approval</u> for the donation of organs. In Italy one of the main obstacles preventing a organ transplant is the refusal of permission for donation of the organs by the patient's relatives.

Current Italian legislation stipulates that organs cannot be removed from a patient if there is a written refusal of the removal from the patient's family or representatives. Unfortunately there are often many reasons behind this refusal to donate organs, including emotional, religious and cultural ones. For all of us interested in carrying out transplant operations in the best possible manner, we are faced with the problem of how to overcome this obstacle. In order to achieve this many have proposed (in our opinion wrongly) to abolish this clause in the current legislation. They say, the doctor should be free, without needing a permission, to carry out the removal of organs when the correct technical conditions exist. The indispensability of the permission is justified by the fact that a social benefit (in this case the availability of organs) always has priority over an individual benefit (in this case the body of the deceased patient).

However, this type of solution to the problem is plainly simplistic and does not take into consideration the fundamental values of tradition, cultural and religious feelings.

No law is capable of overturning, from one day to the next, norms of social behaviour acquired over centuries. Respect for these norms forms the connective tissue of our society.

The problem should be dealt with in a different and more clear-cut way. First of all we must identify the reasons behind this refusal of permission. Contrary to what most people believe, respect for even the sacredness of the body is not the most common reason for opposition to the removal of organs, and only in certain communities does this factor govern refusal to a significant degree. There are, in fact, many other reasons behind this refusal. The first is- without doubt - the lack of knowledge about the true meaning of the term "brain death". Most people doubt that a patient whose heart is still beating is really dead. Furthermore, this doubt is often heightened by the improper use of confusing terms such as: deep coma, irreversible coma, apallic syndrome, peristent vegetative state, and so on. The direct responsability for this can be blamed also on doctors themselves, who all too often release details (to newspapers, radio and television) of miraculous successes of treatment which have led to the more or less complete reawakening of patients who were considered to be in a deep coma for years. Most people do not know the difference between "brain death" and "deep coma" and easily confuse the two terms. A more correct use of the words and the adoption of unambiguous terms would prevent, or at least reduce, the present confusion.

However, if we wish to obtain permission more easily, the first thing to do is to carry out a programme of education which, by using simple terms, clearly explains to the public why brain death means the death of the entire organism. At the same time, we must have the courage to declare that medicine is not able to resuscitate a patient in a state of brain death.

Some people have expressed doubt whether a doctor is able to diagnose with certainty and without the slightest possibility of error that brain death has taken place. This doubt is justified and is strengthened by a lack of uniformity at the international level of clinical and instrumental diagnostic criteria. If we were all to adopt the same criteria and in particular an equal duration for the observation period such doubts would not arise.

Another reason for confusion is caused by the fact that the instrumental therapeutic assistance (life support system) is discontinued more often in those braindeath patients who must be operated for the removal of their organs.

By contrast, there is a futile continuation of respiratory and circulatory assistance until cardiac death ensues in those braindeath patients, whose organs (for whatever reasons) are not required for transplant purposes. This prolongation of treatment is often undertaken so as not to feel directly responsible for the outcome of the patient. All this leads to the believe-among some family members-that the anesthesiologist can still do something to save the life of their relatives.

The problem of permission for a transplant cannot be simply resolved by passing laws. Undoubtedly, this would be the most convenient way, but it would definitely be the least efficent. It would risk causing a more or less open mistrust of doctors by patients' relatives. These people entrust their relatives to us with the conviction that we do all the possible to save the patient's life and this relationship of trust is an indispensable element for a favourable outcome of the treatment. Instead we must try to convince them that we are not enforcing them to give their permission.

To obtain such a positive attitude we can act in the following ways:
- educating the public about the problems connected with organ transplants and the validity of the results achieved through this treatment;
- creation of "ethical committees" in hospitals whose task would be to obtain permission from patients' relatives;
- adoption of uniform criteria at an international level for the diagnosis of brain death;

introduction of legislation which establishes the diagnosis of brain death independently from the removal of organs for transplant purposes and which would allow us to discontinue treatment whenever such a diagnosis is confirmed. It is a painful task to ask relatives to approve a donation of organs, but there is no logical, scientific or human reason to continue treating a body which is no longer alive.

DISCUSSION

Crul: Dr. Manni has presented the difficult task of defining brain death before a transplantation can occur. In our country we have gone through a whole series of stages in which after every few years there was again a new committee nominated to make a newer definition of brain death. The younger the committee was, or the more recent it was, the more sophisticated the means of measurement presented. Nowadays, of course, all the scanning methods and angiography make a more certain diagnosis of brain death, but they also prevent the transplant doctors to use brain dead people at the appropriate time as organ donors. It has always been difficult to handle this in a proper way. On one side the family should feel sure that - when such a decision has been made - the patient is certainly brain dead, but on the other side the body should still be useful for organ transplantation. Have you gone through the same kind of progressively more detailed brain death criteria, Prof. Manni?

Manni: Yes, but sometimes it is difficult to actually do angiography and tomography, as it is necessary to bring the patient to the radiologist's room, in spite of his critical condition. Sometimes we only have a short time, because it is not always possible to maintain organs in an excellent condition necessary for transplantation. In my opinion the critical moment is when the relatives see the patient in the critical care unit. They see the patient's heart beating, but breathing is done by a machine, the blood pressure is maintained by drugs, and the brain is dead. This is the point to make the relatives understand. I think sometimes that all depends on the approach of the intensivist to the relatives of the patient. Relatives are afraid that the intensivist will do something to save the organ and not enough to save the life of the patient. As I said earlier, in my country the mentalities differ. In the north of Italy it is easier for doctors working in the intensive care units using organs than for those in the central region and the south. In the south of Italy the body is sacred. It is not only very difficult to use an organ, but also to do a legal section for pathological reasons. It is necessary to convince the relatives that the patient is really dead.

Crul: The emotional criteria for brain death are, in the eyes of the family, different from those we use for organ transplantation. As long as there is circulation, although combined with artificial ventilation, for them the patient is not yet absolutely dead. We have concentrated ourselves on the brain death as the ultimate criterium, but that does not mean much to people looking at their relatives. They always hope that it is some kind of deep sleep and that

111

the patient will recover as long as the whole body is kept in a reasonable condition, as we do with all our measures.

Manni: In my opinion it is a matter of informing and educating the public.

René: The criteria for brain death do not exist in the French law, although it refers to the opinion of the Academy of Medicine and the Legal Council. Effectively, when the electroencephalogram is flat, the patient is suspected to be brain dead. This is actually the most used criterium, but lately angiography and radioisotope studies are enforced too.

Crul: We do not demand only global death of the cortex, but also of the brain stem. All the cells of the brain should be dead, and that is why we now demand these more extensive criteria. I think that we in principle should still rely on the clinical signs, because without them the more technical signs become too dominant. These special studies should be an addition, like we have the addition of monitoring to the observation by the senses during anaesthesia.

Manni: The main problem arises, when in the case of a young patient as a probable organ donor, we stop the support at an early stage and we take the organs in the operation theatre, with the permission of the relatives, of course. The doctors then say to the relatives the patient was really dead. However, if we have a patient who is 80 years old, whose organs are not suitable for transplantation, we continue to support him/her until the heart arrests. Therefore these patients are treated differently.

Lassner: We do not truly experience these situations as death. In our minds, whether we are doctors or just plain citizens, we have a different attitude to a patient when he has all the appearances of life but is declared dead, then when they start to smell, which is the old criterion of death. If the body decomposes, then he is dead. If we want to use one individual's body to maintain another individual's life, the best model for this is cannibalism. Then you can keep an individual alive by eating the body of another one. This has been done all through the time, even during the last world war, for example. A number of observations exists where slices of muscle tissue have been taken from people who were still alive. They were not strong enough to fight for their lives. Probably these tissues were easier to chew. If we see young people on motor bikes on our streets, who are potential kidney donors, we do not pick them off the bike and take the kidneys out straight away to avoid spending money eventually by keeping them alive, only because we feel they have no brains. Otherwise they would not ride on these bikes. They still have enough of appearance of life and intelligence. We have the same attitude towards people in intensive care units. They have a heart beat, they are rosy thanks to a machine which makes them breath, and you do not feel that they are dead. If you listen to the way even Prof. Manni expresses himself, he switches from "dead body" to "patient" every few minutes or sentence, but a dead body is not a patient anymore. If you consider him as a patient he is not a dead body. This is a very touchy subject in my opinion and quite different from wanting everybody to be used up to the last piece of bone. I have given my hair to science, they can use it after my death. (Note editor: Prof. Lassner is bald).

René: In our country brain death is the only criterium for taking an organ.

Crul: In Holland, when you cannot get the heart to resume its pumping function again, while the patient is on extracorporeal circulation, that is the moment, when we decide to ask the relatives if we may use the patient as organ donor. I do not know how it is in other countries.

Hargrove: May I make two points. I think that Prof. Manni has got it absolutely right that you must educate people to understand what you are trying to do as far as organ transplantation is concerned. We have a slightly different attitude to brain death in that we do turn off the ventilator on all patients before we declare them dead. We do not just turn it off on those who are going to be organ donors. We involve the relatives in the decision-making process by asking them to come and see the tests done. The tests in England have to be done by two independent consultant doctors and the relatives have to be able to see what is being done. We do not do angiography at all. It is not necessary for o r diagnosis of brain death.

Manni: Is it necessary in your country when you want to take organs to have the permission of the relatives?

Hargrove: There is a move to suggest that you ought to be able to opt out of the scheme, in other words, if someone is severely damaged you take the organs without permission. That has not come yet. For the benefit of Mrs. Palay-Vincent, we had an interesting medico-legal problem regarding this. A man had been severely assaulted, got severe brain damage, was taken into the intensive care unit, and after four days the ventilator was turned off. The man, who was charged with the murder of this patient said "No, the murder took place in the intensive care unit". He left the patient with his heart still beating, and therefore it was the doctors who were guilty of the murder and not himself. It was a very neat legal point. He lost.

Lassner: There is a similar situation which arises quite frequently in France, when an anaesthetic accident has occurred. The patient is not dead, but in coma. Then someone feels that if he would have been treated better in the intensive care unit, he would even have survived. His death is not directly due to the accident, but to the poor care he received afterwards. This has been kept quiet in several cases quite effectively.

Hallèn: I agree with all of you that a lot of education is necessary, and I feel myself as a doctor in need of education in this matter. In my country a parliamentary committee has been trying to study these problems. Probably we will have a bill this autumn on how to decide when a person is dead. In my view it is still very confusing. When the body and soul are no longer kept together we have to decide when the individual is dead, not when mere parts of that body - which were part of the individual - are dead. There arises at least one intriguing legal finesse.

Perhaps the lawyers could give me an answer to the question of who owns a body. Is it an individual owning some property, and when that individual no longer exists who can own the mere shell of that individual? Your possessions of an individual are immediately transferred to your heirs, that is for sure, but is there actually a law in any country saying who owns the body? This is important, because we are sort of faking things for ourselves by just using words. I would like to remember the words of R. Kipling, who said that words are the most powerful drug known to mankind. We are intoxicating ourselves by using the word donor, that means "give". "Give" is an active action that has to be done by an individual, and how can a dead person be a donor? That is one way we are blinding ourselves.

Palay-Vincent: This problem was posed to the court when two years ago we had the problem of postmortem insemination. We had to question, whose property is the sperm when a man is dead. If the court says the sperm is a "good", then it can be appropriated by anyone in the family. For the sperm, the question posed was: "Can the parents inherit the sperm?", but the tribunal said they could not, because it is not a "good". Some people then said: "But what about organs?" I always answer, that for the organs it is necessary to have a law. In France is a law for organ donors now, but for the sperm we have no law, so we cannot compare it. We cannot say, for instance, that sperm is an organ, so we can give it to someone, it is not. We discussed this matter about the sperm in front of the tribunal.

Lassner: Is this difference made because one can compare sperm to urine as being secreted from the body, or is it part of the body? If you consider it part of the body, and thus nobody's belonging, and - if I understand you correctly - the body does not belong to anybody, so how can you dispose of it rightfully? If you want to take a pencil one would say it does not belong to you. Does this body belong to nobody and anybody can take parts of it?

Palay-Vincent: Before the law you cannot dispose of it, because your body does not belong to you after death, and we need a law to derogate it.

Lassner: Dr. Hallèn properly said, that the term "organ donor" is a misnomer, the organs are taken away, the person did not "give" them. Donor is one who gives, so "organ donor" is a contradiction in terms. On the other hand, the question now comes up of who could give the organ.

Crul: The dead body is more like an organ "stock", not a donor.

René: In France organs are out of trade: it is impossible to sell an organ.

Lassner: This was settled for blood 50 years ago. You cannot buy or sell blood in France. It is part of the body and is not for sale. You can compensate the blood donor for his travel, but you cannot buy it from him.

René: An exception is maternal milk. Women are considered like cows for milk.

Roos: In Holland, I think, you can speak of a real donor, because you only have the right to take organs from a brain dead person after the person has written a codicil while alive, allowing the donation of some or all of his or her organs after his or her death. When the law threatens to be changed as such, that you have to write a negative codicil to protect your organs from being taken out after death, the situation gets totally different, of course. This is the case in Belgium.

Wroblewski: In Germany we are trying to construct a kind of patient's last will. If we do not have it done directly by the patient, we try to get it from the family, and then construct a will. Another point is that several years ago in Germany we had a legal initiative - similar to what is prepared in Belgium now -, that if you do not want to be an organ donor, you have to mention it in your papers. If you do not do it, automatically you are assumed to be willing to be an organ donor. It was not accepted politically. We have basically a medical rule for organ donors. I think there will not be any great opposition to find a common opinion. What gives us problems are more political questions and mistrust by the patient's family. We therefore do a lot of protective medicine in order to keep the neighbours and the world quiet, and perhaps sometimes we overdo this procedure, just from the political point of view.

Hargrove: I can answer Dr. Hallèn's point from the United Kingdom's viewpoint. When a patient dies, when they are certified dead, the body becomes the property of the relatives, and as such they have the legal responsibility to dispose of that property. They have to bury it or dispose of it in another way, cremation, or by organ donation, so in fact the donation is by the relatives rather than by the ex-patient, as the body is the property of the relatives.

116

Roos: In Holland the patient has the ultimate word as to whether the body should be used for organ transplantation or not. The body does not become the property of the relatives afterwards, but the relatives or the inheritors have the duty to dispose of the body within the legal boundaries. They may not get any benefit from it, as it is not their property, but they also must not treat it disrespectfully. Their responsibility is to bury or cremate the body within the legal boundaries.

Palay-Vincent: I think this is the same for us. There is no property on the body.

Lassner: I would like to tell you a legal difficulty, arising out of this. Who has to pay for transportation of a dead individual from one hospital to another? This occurred on the frontier of the country between France and Switzerland, where dead bodies were transported to Geneva to be used as organ donors. The various organisms in charge of transporting the patients - ambulance service and so on - asked to be paid for transporting them. There were no provisions to do so, because the various social security arrangements provided only money for transporting patients within the country. For obvious reasons they also could not be transported in the funeral van as really dead bodies. Corpses are only carried in ambulances after accidents and then only incidentally.

RULES OF PROCEDURES FOR ANAESTHESIOLOGISTS IN CASE OF FAULTS OR (NEAR) ACCIDENTS

J.F. Crul

I think we should now draw our attention to the last question to be discussed being the proposition we should give anaesthetists and what they should do after accidents or faults have occurred. It is my experience, that the way anaesthetists behave after an accident or fault have occurred, has sometimes made their case more difficult. Either they have not dealt with it in such a way that the court could come to a clear conclusion, or the conclusion would have been more favourable for the anaesthetist, if he had conducted himself in a more proper and clear way after the accident had happened. Therefore, I feel it is very useful to hear from this group what we should propose to anaesthetists around Europe what to do or not after serious accidents. Many hospitals in most countries now have a so-called FONA committee. FONA means "faults or near-accidents" committee. The individual specialist has to inform the FONA committee after an accident or a near-accident has occurred, to make sure that all the facts are properly and completely collected. If a lawsuit should come out of it these data can be used in court. In Holland most hospitals have such a FONA committee. Of course, before discussing this subject, we must clearly define the term "fault", "accident" and "near-accident". In the Dutch Society of Anesthesiology we have composed such definitions. We discussed them with some legal advisers in Holland and came to definitions as stated below:

A "fault" is an accusable action or negligence on behalf of the anaesthetist or his assistant(s) causing damage to a patient. So it is a clear accusable action or negligence in relation to the damage caused to a patient.

An "accident" we have defined as every fact causing damage to a patient or his death with no guilt on the part of the anaesthetist as long as this fact is not included in a previously calculated and consciously taken risk. It is a damage occurring to the patient without the intention of it being a risk taken consciously by the anaesthetist, and intended by him for the good of the patient. In many English speaking countries accidents are part of "mishaps", being considered something different from what could be expected or predicted.

A "near accident" we define as something usually having led to a fault or an accident, but which did not happen by reasons which are not under the command of the anaesthetist or his assistents.

Since the question of "guilt" cannot be answered right away at the moment such an act or fact occurs, we have proposed to compile rules for the anaesthetist to use whenever one of these three things happen: faults, accidents and near-accidents.

Documentation, Information, Data collection.

These three are important to have available in case an act or a fact involving damage to a patient leads to a lawsuit. I have included for all of you a kind of outline of the different things necessary for this documentation, information, and data collection. In my experience as an expert witness over the last 10-15 years, the most frequent causes of problems in a law court happened, when these documents and data are lacking or not organised properly. Many cases led to conviction just by the pure fact, that documents were not available, had disappeared, had been changed afterwards, or had not been given at all or very scarcely.

The Dutch Society of Anesthesiology has recently published these general rules for their membership. It may be helpful for the members of the European Society of Anesthesiologists to read this set of rules from the Dutch Society. They are divided in three categories:

A. Documentation

All the facts concerning the mishap should be registered fully and in a correct time frequence. They include:

A full list of preoperative conditions and premedication. Dosages and types of medication for induction and maintenance. Important surgical events (bleeding, opening of cavities, clamping or servering of large vessels, nerves or intestines). Vital organ functions (respiration circulation and central nervous system). The use of monitoring instruments and the readings respectively their recordings.

These documents together with the complete description of the patients' condition should principely be given to the director of the hospital and submitted to the Hospital (near) Accidents Committee (FONA committee).

B. Information

Full information of the events has to be given to:
the chairman of the department, the medical director of the hospital, the accidents committee of the hospital. If deemed necessary by the first two authorities, also information should be given to: the patient or (if deceased) his/her family. The medical staff of the hospital (medical audit), the general practioner of the patient, the anaesthesiologist's or the hospital's insurance company. In case of death or maior bodily harm also to: the regional health inspector and the state attorney.
In no circumstances should the question of guilt be raised.

C. Witnesses and pieces of evidence (proofs).

They include the following:
names and written testimonies of witnesses of the mishaps. All aparatus, vials, equipment and other material should be isolated and kept ready for inspection by authorities and experts.
If a post mortem is done, the anaesthesiologist involved in a case should (if allowed) be present to give background information and ask for special investigations (f.i. chemical or microscopic).
The case should be discussed extensively in the staff meeting of the anaesthesia department and, if possible, include the other specialists involved. All these activities should be focussed on the prevention of future recur ences.

There are still a few additional things I would like to remark at this point. In the witnesses and proofs section I would like to add two points of interest:
1. One person should be the central point for communications with legal and press agents, particularly in more serious cases as otherwise all people will start giving witness, which can cause a very confusing situation. Even people not directly involved may start giving all kinds of judgements and so cause unjustified rumours;
2. The matter of guilt should be left out systematically by all people involved in the hospital or in the case. This was expressed long ago in Latin: "Nemo teneto si ipsum acquisare", which means: "Don't accuse yourself too soon". Although it seems a bit mean to do so, it is still very valid in all kinds of possibilities of legal actions, that nobody in the hospital, neither the

director nor the chief of the department nor the other specialist involved, should say a single word about guilt of someone in such a case.

DISCUSSION

Wroblewski: We have to separate two conceptions: fault and accident. By fault we mean that it is accusable. This is an opinion expressed by the judge. The only thing we are forced to do as specialists is to keep facts. Your procedure, Prof. Crul, is right, "nemo teneto" as you mentioned before. In criminal law this means no one is forced to accuse himself. If you go so far as to say it is a fault, in criminal law that would mean that you accuse yourself, but nobody forces you to do so. I think we should rule out everything which tends to be an opinion. We can only present facts, present the documentation, but no opinion, because our opinions might be wrong. In our legal system it is solely up to the judge to give opinions, and he forms his opinion from facts.

Lassner: In France it also extends to the expert witness; the expert witness is not to judge, he is not to say that it is a faulty way of acting, he may only say that it is or is not in conformity with actual practice, that it seems to be or not a mistake in interpretoring a sign, or that the dosage applied does not seem adequate or appropriate for the case. The question of fault belongs to the judge.

Crul: The expert witness can only make clear to the judge what the standard of care would be in a comparable situation given by the average specialist in a similar setting.

Lassner: These standards of care are not the same in a remote part of the country as they are in the university hospital.

Crul: That is a frequent fault made by expert witnesses. In Holland, the expert witnesses are usually chosen from university departments and they compare the situation in a general hospital with a situation in their own very sophisticated circumstances. They then condemn the anaesthetist on the basis of this false comparison. The case should always be compared to that of a general anaesthetist in the same kind of circumstances.

Lassner: There is one point which I would like to take up with Dr. Wroblewski. I read in a German journal recommendations by suggesting that after an accident the anaesthetist should not give any statement, no self-accusation is requested. I do not think that this could hold in France. The inquiry in France is initially a police inquiry, the people involved are giving testimony, and if you refuse testimony you are probably acting against the law, because giving testimony is an obligation. What would our French lawyers say to this? If a doctor, who was asked about a patient found dead in his office, said "I do not know, I will not say anything", is the doctor not likely to be arrested for possibly having murdered that patient?

René: The legal situation in France is such that the law on secrecy of profession does not permit a doctor to give any statement, certainly not in front of a police investigator and even if he is asked in front of the tribunal by the judge he has first to say he is not permitted to testify because he is obliged to follow the legal prescription of secrecy in profession. The doctor may not divulge secrets, known to him through his profession.

Wroblewski: In Germany he may.

René: There is one exception to the prescription of secrecy in profession. Once a penal procedure is on its way, the judge can seize all the documents and he can designate an expert - who must be a doctor - and he askes the doctor concerned to provide the expert information.

Lassner: There is another word which has not been mentioned. As long as a doctor is not accused, he has no access to claims and to the contents of the case. If he wants to know what it is all about, he has to ask the judge to accuse him officially, then his lawyer will have access to the documents.

Crul: That is the same in Holland.

Wroblewski: It is different in Germany. You cannot ask a judge to accuse you. The prosecutor must accuse someone if certain rules are breached. I think in Germany you have the right to refuse testimony, if there is a danger of self-accusation. We also have to separate two matters. We are now talking about judicial consequences and not about ethical and moral questions. I think it will be ethical and moral to help to bring the truth to the surface, but in judicial settings you do not have to do this. The only thing the state prosecutor can do, is to prove guilt in procedural legal means, and the lawyer has to watch that the prosecutor and all the state organs are just proving guilt by procedurally accepted means. That means you are not forced to accuse or to do anything to prove your guilt.

Crul: I would like to ask Dr. Hargrove and Dr. Hallèn to give their recommendations for rules in such situations. Dr. Hargrove, who works in the medical defence union, would you feel that setting up such rules or recommendations for doctors, when they have accidents, would be reasonable, or do you have some objections?

Hargrove: I do not speak for the Medical Defence Union, and certainly I could not speak for the other defence bodies. What I would like to do is to take this document back and talk to the people in my defence society to see whether they would approve of this sort of thing.

Hallèn: I would say this paper is very much along the lines our investigations go after we have complaints. As you have heard our system is rather different from those on the continent, so all cases of this type are filed with the authorities and then we perform an investigation very much along these lines. This goes very well with the way I recommend my colleagues to proceed. As soon as something happens, do take notes of everything, do make written reports from all persons involved, and file them for your own safety. If something comes up afterwards, there is much more reliance on those papers written immediately than on those produced later on, while the legal proceedings are going on. Apart from the variations as to people involved, names, etc., I would say that this would suit us very well.

Wroblewski: To me it looks as being too many people involved in this information. I would agree with the head of the department of anaesthesia, the director of the hospital, who is purely an administrator in Germany, but all the others seem to me to be excessive. I think in strictly judicial categories, it sounds just a little too close to self-accusation and it creates a bad atmosphere, a kind of prejudice against the doctor. We have to keep it quiet without trying to cover it up.

Crul: I can understand how you feel about this. Of course, these rules are set up for serious things, not for minor accidents.

Lassner: As a closing remark, in France we are asked to inform our insurance companies in writing on the day it happened. In public hospitals the administration also acts without delay because they insure themselves, they are their own insurance company, and they must be advised.

Crul: In Holland almost all hospitals have an insurance policy which includes everyone practising in that hospital. The insurance company is informed by the director of the hospital.

Hallèn: Under C. of your rules and procedures, the anaesthetist involved should be present to give the background information and to ask for a special investigation. It seems to me a bit too far going because then all the other people can be asked by the judge, by the prosecutor, what was said. In this way you can undermine his legal position and it is a kind of self-accusation.

ANAESTHESIOLOGICAL RESPONSIBILITIES FOR THE DAY-CARE PATIENT

C. Roos

Anaesthesiologists have the moral and legal responsibility to treat each of their patients with an optimal and recognized standard of care. This care has to be given in the pre-, per- and post-operative period.

In clinical patients the anaesthesiologist delegates a certain part of this care, especially postoperatively, to other qualified medical personnel, i.e. ward-physicians and ward-nurses. However, she/he retains the ultimate responsibility for at least 24 hours postoperatively.

In the case of a day-care patient, the anaesthesiologist also retains this ultimate responsibility for 24 hours, but will delegate part of it to the patients and their caretakers.

Since we must assume that they are no skilled in medicis, the anaesthesiologist adds specific areas of responsiblity to her/his own moral and legal tasks. These specific areas can be seen as:

I   The selection of the type of the operative procedure, suitable for day-care surgery.

II   The selection of the patients suited for day-care anaesthesia, not only medically but also psycho-socially.

III   The standard of the anaesthesiological facilities during the operation and the pre- and postoperative period.

IV   The selection of the anaesthesiological pharmaceuticals.

V   The assessment of the patients streetfitness.

VI   The Instructions to the patients, their caretakers and extramural medical personnel, whom the day-care patients may consult. ^ @

I. The selection of the postoperative procedure

Normally, the unspoken contract between patient and doctor is based on the obligation to give the best possible care, but does not garantee a good result. Since the choice of the procedure for day-care surgery is based on a low complication and high success rate of the operation, the day-care patient has the right to expect an even more successful outcome than in-patients. In unsuccessful outcome or serious complications it can be a hard case for surgeon and anaesthetist to prove that the adverse result is not due to a lacking standard of care.

Generally, those types of surgery are suitable for day-care which are elective, short, have few or no complications, require no blood transfusion or postoperative intravenous drugs, do not give severe postoperative pain which requires opiates, do not necessitate intensive nursing (e.g. wounddressing) and allow patients to resume their normal life pattern (included eating and drinking) within 24 hours.

In many surgical and anaesthesiological studies it has been shown, that mortality and morbidity are dependent on the type and the length of the surgery performed. The least number of complications is seen in surgery of the extremities (mortality 0,2%), cystoscopy (0,6%), curettages (0,1%) and inquinal herniorraphy (0,4%). Most complications are seen in intracranial (17,8%), intrathoracic (18,1%), abdominal (13,3%) and tracheal/laryngeal surgery (37,8%). So, upper airway surgery, apart from adenotomy and tonsillectomy is not suitable for daycare surgery. The same goes for surgery, where cranum, thoracical or abdominal cavities are opened. Statistically the duration of the surgery is directly proportional to the number of postoperative complications (0,5% at 30 minutes, 4% in 2 hours). A tendency to perform invasive radiological procedures under anaesthesia in a day-care setting is increasing. However, these procedures have a higher rate of complications, especially allergic complications than minor surgery!

II. The selection of the patients

The ASA-score, as an estimate of health or disease, is a well-known and trustworthy tool in the hands of the anaesthesiologist. ASA I and II patients have an overall morbidity of less than 6% in anaesthesia for day-care surgery. ASA III: approx. 10%, ASA IV: approx. 14%, ASA V: approx. 25%. For this reason only ASA I en ASA II patients can safely be accepted as day-care patients. Acute or emergency surgery has a greater anaesthesiological morbidity and mortality and is therefore not suitable.

Children can be accepted for day-care surgery, when they are over 6 months of age. Ex-premature patients must be over 1 year of age. Elderly patients can be accepted as day-care patients, if their physical, mental and socio-economic situations allows this.

All day-care patients must want to have their surgery done as day-care patients. It may never be forced upon them! The patient must be able to understand the instructions and be willing and able to carry them out. For instance: removal of osteosynthesis material from an ankle can be done as a day-care procedure in a patient, who lives with relatives in a ground-floor appartment, but not in a patient who lives alone in a fourth-floor appartment without elevator. It is the anaesthesiologist's responsibility to assess the psycho-social circumstances in each patient, who is proposed for day-care anaesthesia. The anaesthesiologist should thereby take into account, that patients with poor intelligence and/or social circumstances can be less assertive in stating their needs towards the physician.

III, Per-operative facilities
The day-care patient should be anaesthesized and recover surrounded by the same standard of care and monitoring as any comparable clinical patient. If day-care surgery is performed in the "normal" O.R.'s, this seldom creates a problem. However, in the set-up of a special day-care surgery centre, it is the anaesthesiologist's duty to ensure that O.R.'s and recovery rooms have all the necessary facilities to monitor and to treat any possible complication. Failure to establish this is not only lack in patient-care, but is also a part of the anaesthesiologist's legal responsibility.
The postoperative day-care unit should also have "ward-facilities", i.e. food and drinks for patients, a waiting area for relatives, and so on.
Although few the expected complications in day-care surgery, the opportunity to admit a patient to proper clinical care must always be available in a day-care organisation.

IV. Selection of anaesthesia-pharmaceuticals
Various techniques for safe conductance of day-care anaesthesia with short-acting drugs and techniques have been widely described in the litterature. Familiarity with these techniques and conducting anaesthesia in accordance with the approved methods is part of the anaesthesiologist's moral and legal responsibility.

V. Assessment of streetfitness
No day-care patient should leave the hospital without the personal O.K. of the anaesthesiologist. Streetfitness can be assessed in many different ways. Since anaesthesia affects difference systems, a.o. motor-skills, coordination of eye-movement, intellectual performance, (circulatory) autoregulation, all these systems must be checked before releasing the patient.
Very sophisticated and expensive gadgets have been brought on the market for this purpose, but pen and paper, a maddox-wing, a rubber ball (to bounce and catch) are cheap, easy to handle and relatively trustworthy. Important is, that different systems are objectivily tested and that not the patients' and/or the nurses' statements that "everything is fine" is taken for granted.

Objective testing is good patient-care, but also a legal protection for the anaesthesiologist, especially when performed in the presence of a nurse or assistant and recorded on a streetfitness-checklist.

VI. Instructions to patients, caretakers and other (para)medical personnel

For day-care patients and their caretakers a leaflet (see next) can be helpful and may be seen as a minimum care tool. Even if the leaflet comes with an informed consent part which the patient is required to sign, it will never replace the duty of the anaesthesiologist to interview and instruct each patient and/or caretaker verbally. It can be very helpfull, if the day-care centre and especially the anaesthesiologists develop instructions for G.P.'s and district-nurses in their area. Mostly the complaints which can be expected are minor anaesthesiological sequellae like nausea, fatigue, sore throat or dizziness. Although an obligatory and integral part of a day-care centre is 24-hour-availability of an anaesthesiologist for consultation and treatment of possible complications, some patients will turn to their G.P.'s and/or district-nurses.

Good rules for communication between the day-care centre and the regional extramural medical profession will make handling of day-care patients safer, and will make G.P.'s and district nurses more able and willing to take part in optimal care for day-care patients.

CONCLUSION

The best and most responsible care for patients in a day-care setting is given by competent, involved anaesthesiologists assisted by good technical facilities in a well-organised setting. A day-care anaesthesia set-up can be a good example of the widening surroundings of the anaesthesiologists' tasks. Their duties reach out from the boundaries of the day-care into the patients homes.

The least anaesthesilogical morbidity will occur when the anaesthesiologists consider their day-care patients as their own patients.

Day-care anaesthesia. A model of an information leaflet for patients

General information
- Your surgical specialist has advised you to have your surgical/diagnostical procedure and your anaesthesia as a day-care patient.
- Day-care surgery means, that you arrive at the day-care centre in the morning and return home the same day.

- You are supposed to arrive with an empty stomach, which means that you have not eaten or drunk anything after 24.00 hrs the preceeding day.
- The day-care centre is located   ----------------------
  and has telephone number   ----------------------
  Accompagning relatives can stay   ----------------------

Advise
A - Pre-operative
- Bring your hospital-card and insurance card with you.
- Stop smoking from now on.
- Do not drink alcoholic beverages at least 24 hours prior to the procedure.
- Ask your surgical specialist before the procedure for a prescription for paintreatment.
- If you use any medication, please bring them with you to the hospital and show them to the anaesthetist. It is important that the anaesthetist is accurately informed about your medication and your social habits (smoking, drinking, drugs).
- Inform your anaesthetist accurately on:
  1. your state of health
  2. previous experiences of anaesthesia of you and your family
  3. previous blood transfusions
  4. the state of your teeth, including dentures
  5. tatoos
  6. previous living or working abroad.
- Women, who use anticonceptive pills should continue to do so during the period of the anaesthesia, but are advised not to consider themselves fully protected for the remainder of the cycle in which the procedure takes place.
- Shower or bathe thoroughly before arriving at the day-care centre.
- Do not use any aspirine-like drugs at least a week before the procedure. Switch to other painkillers, if necessary. When you take aspirine as a precaution against myocardial or cerebral infarction, do not stop using them. Inform the anaesthetist. An extra bloodtest might be necessary.
- Do not wear make-up. Remove all traces of make-up and nailpolish carefully.
- Remove contactlenses, dentures, hearing-aids or any other protheses before the procedure.
- Do not wear any jewelry. The hospital declines responsibility for your valuables. Please leave them at home.

B - postoperative
- You are not allowed to go home:
  a. by public transport
  b. driving your own means of transport
  c. alone.
  Take care that you provide company before!
- Do not use public transport for at least 36 hours.
- Do not drive or ride any vehicle for at least 36 hours.
- Stay at home at least 36 hours, rest as much as possible and eat only small, light meals.
- Do not use any alcoholic beverage during at least 36 hours. Your alcohol tolerance can be impaired for at least a week.
- Do not use any sharp objects or tools for at least 36 hours (sewing machines, sawing machines, scissors, karving knives).
- Do not take important decisions for at least 36 hours.
- Do not stay alone for 24 hours after the procedure.
- It is normal that you are more quickly tired for approx. one week. Please arrange no long-distance travels or tiring meetings in this week.

Complaints after the procedure
- Your may have a sore throat, muscle pains and/or wound pains during several days.
- Light headedness or dizziness can occur at sudden changes in position.
- Emotional stability can be less than normal for some days after anaesthesia.

If you experience other complaints after the procedure, please call the anaesthetist on call number --------. There is always (24 out of 24 hours) an anaesthetist available on this number.

Lastly
- Your G.P. is informed about the procedure and your status as a day-care patient.
- You will leave the hospital in a wheelchair.
- All advises are also for patients who receive any form of local or regional anaesthesia, combined with sedation.
- Being a day-care patient means, that you are able and willing to take responsibility for your own health after the procedure.
  Please sign the following paper and hand it over to your anaesthetist.

- I agree to undergo ------------------------------- (name procedure) under anaesthesia as a day-care patient.
- I have read and understood all the advised.
- I am able and willing to follow the advises.

(Signature of patient)

GENERAL CONCLUSIONS

J.F. Crul

Legal basis of anaesthesia mishaps are based on similar grounds throughout the countries of Western Europe. This common denominator is probably the Napoleontic lawcode, which spread over Europe at the end of the 19th century.
The division into civil, penal and disciplinary lawcode can be seen in all of them. Also the differentiation into the two main grounds for civil liability, namely "malpractice" and "breach of care" can be seen in all juridical procedures. Differences in approaches can be noticed in:
. rules of procedure
. burden of proof
. magistrates or committees involved
. individual versus team liabilities
. informed consent
. standards of care.
Legal actions against anaesthesiologists are on the increase also in Europe. They have both positive and negative effects.
On the positive side they make the anaesthesiologists more aware of the specific responsibilities of their profession and the do's and don't's to avoid legal repercussions of anaesthesia mishaps, and the steps to take when these mishaps lead to serious damage of the patient. An improvement of the standards of care by anaesthesiologists is the additional benefit emerging from all these legal actions.
On the negative side has to be mentioned the fear for reprisals and the introduction of some form of "defensive medicine" also in anaesthesia. This last danger is already real in some states of the U.S.A., because of the high number of legal steps taken against anaesthesiologists.
An increasing tendency exists amongst patients in some European countries to choose the easy and cheap way of filing a penal case against an anaesthetist and if they succeed, to seek recompensation by a civil procedure.

The second half of this book showes the great diversity in legal implications of the modern involvement of anaesthesia in many fields of intensive and emergency medicine as well as organ transplantation. Separation from ethical questions becomes less and less clear and enforces us to reenact our standards in this field as well.

With exception of Sweden, where the legal cases are carefully registered, there is a clear lack of information on the frequency of the legal problems in anaesthesia in relation to the practice of anaesthesia for the rest of the European countries. An identical multinational registration in the countries of the European Community would enable the European Academy of Anaesthesiology to make an inventory of the extent of the legal consequences of their profession.

When in 1992 all countries of the E.C. will be united into one Europe, it is likely that also the standards of care in anaesthesia, as they are used in legal cases for comparison with the conduct of the individual anaesthetist, will become more and more uniform.

Informing anaesthesiologists on what to expect in the way of legal consequences in their profession is the main purpose of this book.

DEVELOPMENTS IN CRITICAL CARE MEDICINE AND ANESTHESIOLOGY

1. Prakash, O. (ed.): Applied Physiology in Clinical Respiratory Care. 1982.
   ISBN 90–247–2662–X.
2. McGeown, Mary G.: Clinical Management of Electrolyte Disorders. 1983.
   ISBN 0–89838–559–8.
3. Stanley, T.H., and Petty, W.C. (eds.): New Anesthetic Agents, Devices and Monitoring
   Techniques. 1983. ISBN 0–89838–566–0.
4. Scheck, P.A., Sjöstrand, U.H., and Smith, R.B. (eds.): Perspectives in High Frequency
   Ventilation. 1983. ISBN 0–89838–571–7.
5. Prakash, O. (ed.): Computing in Anesthesia and Intensive Care. 1983.
   ISBN 0–89838–602–0.
6. Stanley, T.H., and Petty, W.C. (eds.): Anesthesia and the Cardiovascular System. Annual
   Utah Post-graduate Course in Anesthesilogy. 1984. ISBN 0–89838–626–8.
7. van Kleef, J.W., Burm, A.G.L., and Spierdijk, J. (eds.): Current Concepts in Regional
   Anaesthesia. 1984. ISBN 0–89838–644–6.
8. Prakash, O. (ed.): Critical Care of the Child. 1984. ISBN 0–89838–661–6.
9. Stanley, T.H., and Petty, W.C. (eds.): Anesthesiology: Today and Tomorrow. Annual Utah
   Post-graduate Course in Anesthesiology. 1985. ISBN 0–89838–705–1.
10. Rahn, H., and Prakash, O. (eds.): Acid-base Regulation and Body Temperature. 1985.
    ISBN 0–89838–708–6.
11. Stanley, T.H., and Petty, W.C. (eds.): Anesthesiology. Annual Utah Post-graduate Course
    in Anesthesiology. 1986.
    ISBN 0–89838–779–5.
12. de Lange, S., Hennis, P.J., and Kettler, D. (eds.): Cardiac Anaesthesia: Problems and
    Innovations. 1986. ISBN 0–89838–794–9.
13. de Bruijn, N.P., and Clements, F.M.: Transesophageal Echocardiography. 1987.
    ISBN 0–89838–821–X.
14. Graybar, G.B., and Bready, L.L. (eds.): Anesthesia for Renal Transplantation. 1987.
    ISBN 0–89838–837–6.
15. Stanley, T.H., and Petty, W.C. (eds.): Anesthesia, the Heart and the Vascular System.
    Annual Utah Postgraduate Course in Anesthesiology. 1987. ISBN 0–89838–851–1.
16. Ronai, A.K.: Autologous Blood Transfusions. 1988. ISBN 0–89838–899–6.
17. Stanley, T.H. (ed.): What's New in Anesthesiology. Annual Utah Postgraduate Course in
    Anesthesiology. 1988. ISBN 0–89838–367–6.
18. Woerlee, G.M.: Common Perioperative Problems and the Anaesthetist. 1988.
    ISBN 0–89838–402–8.
19. Stanley, T.H., and Sperry, R.J. (eds.): Anesthesia and the Lung. 1989.
    ISBN 0–7923–0075–0.
20. De Castro, J., Meynadier, J., and Zenz, M.: Regional Opiod Analgesia.
    Physiopharmacological Basis, Drugs, Equipement and Clinical Application. 1989.
    ISBN 0–7923–0162–5.
21. Crul, J.F. (ed.): Legal Aspects of Anaesthesia. 1989. ISBN 0–7923–0393–8.
22. Freye, E. (ed.), Cerebral Monitoring in the Operating Room and the Intensive Care Unit.
    (In prep.) ISBN 0–7923–0349–X